Series / Number 03-024

Public Administration and the Legislative Process

ALAN P. BALUTIS
State University of New York at Buffalo

JAMES J. HEAPHEY
State University of New York at Albany

⑤ SAGE PUBLICATIONS / Beverly Hills / London

Copyright © 1974 by Sage Publications, Inc.

Printed in the United States of America

All rights reserved. No part of this book may be reproduced or utilized in any form or by any means, electronic or mechanical, including photocopying, recording, or by any information storage and retrieval system, without permission in writing from the publisher.

For information address:

SAGE PUBLICATIONS, INC.
275 South Beverly Drive
Beverly Hills, California 90212

SAGE PUBLICATIONS LTD
St George's House / 44 Hatton Garden
London EC1N 8ER

International Standard Book Number 0-8039-0459-2

Library of Congress Catalog Card No. 74-19987

FIRST PRINTING

When citing a professional paper, please use the proper form. Remember to cite the correct Sage Professional Paper series title and include the paper number. One of the two following formats can be adapted (depending on the style manual used):

(1) OSTROM, E. et al. (1973) "Community Organization and the Provision of Police Services." Sage Professional Papers in Administrative and Policy Studies, 1, 03-001. Beverly Hills and London: Sage Pubns.

OR

(2) Ostrom, Elinor, et al. 1973 *Community Organization and the Provision of Police Services.* Sage Professional Papers in Administrative and Policy Studies, vol. 1, series no. 03-001. Beverly Hills and London: Sage Publications.

JK
3471
B32

CONTENTS

I. Introduction 5
II. Professional Staffing and Conventional Wisdom 10
III. The Functions of the Staff 12
    Intelligence 12
    Integration 22
    Innovation 33
    Influence 39
IV. Summary 51
    Notes 52
    References 56

Public Administration and the Legislative Process

ALAN P. BALUTIS
State University of New York (Buffalo)

JAMES J. HEAPHEY
State University of New York (Albany)

INTRODUCTION

The burgeoning importance of state legislatures is evidenced by the staggering increases in state spending over the past 25 years. Since 1950, state government expenditures have increased 470%—from $15 billion to over $85 billion. Enactment of general revenue sharing and proposals for special revenue sharing, "bloc grants," and other proposals indicate that the future will probably see states receiving more federal money, with greater flexibility as to how they spend these funds. The number and complexity of programs operated by state governments have, similarly, risen sharply during this period, particularly during the past decade.

In spite of this, state legislatures remain, as Alan Rosenthal (1973: 55) has noted, "neglected institutions of American government." Rosenthal points out that during a recent biennium Congress spent some $630 million on itself, for 535 members in two houses. During the same period state legislatures spent about $350 million on themselves, for 7,600 members in 99 houses. He points out further that the imbalance extends to intellectual concern with legislatures. From 1960 to 1971 some 185 articles on legislatures were published in the *American Political Science Review*, the *Journal of Politics*, the *Midwest Journal of Political Science*, and the *Western Political Quarterly*. Of these, 63% focused on Congress, the remainder on state legislatures. During the same period there were 180 doctoral dissertations completed on legislatures. Sixty-six percent of them were on Congress, while the remainder focused on state legislatures.

In this paper we study the role that staff plays in the New York State Legislature by examining that legislature as a working organization and ascertaining how staff affects it as such. We take here an approach familiar to scholars and practitioners in the field of public administration; we study the legislature as a government institution with tasks to perform and objectives to be achieved. We are concerned with how staff plays a part in the workload of that institution. Our purpose is to provide some tentative answers to the following query: Granted, everyone agrees that legislatures should be better staffed to do their work, but what difference does staff make?

We believe that a public administration approach, particularly organization theory, is called for in this study. Legislatures are not normally considered to be within the purview of public administration, except to be cursed or, at best, looked upon as another obstacle confronting the executive. Public administration specialists, even political scientists, have, as Dwight Waldo puts it, regarded themselves rather exclusively as "executive men." The only major figure in the history of American public administration who tried seriously and at great length to have it otherwise was W. F. Willoughby. In the early 1930s Willoughby published three major treatises at the Institute for Government Research, which he directed from 1916 to 1932. The first was titled *Principles of Public Administration*; the second, *Principles of Judicial Administration*; and the third, *Principles of Legislative Organization and Administration*. He sought, he said (1934: v), to examine these three great branches of government "for the purpose of determining the principles that govern, or ought to govern, them in respect to their organization and procedural processes." Willoughby went on to state:

> One does not, at first, view the legislative branch as one presenting problems of administration. Examination, however, shows that it does so to a scarcely less extent than do the other two branches. Here, too, are encountered practical problems of organization, personnel and procedure analogous to those presented by the other two branches and the manner in which they are handled determines to an equal extent the efficiency with which the functions assigned to it are performed.

Willoughby's vision for the field of public administration, continuing study and improvement of the organization and procedures of all three branches of government, was not adopted. Instead, Leonard D. White, who focused solely on the executive branch of government in his monumentally successful introductory text, *Introduction to the Study of Public Administration*, prevailed. The field of public administration became exclusively executive oriented.

White appeared to modify his view in later years. In 1945, he said (1945: 1) that "the next major development in the improvement of administration depends on reform of American legislatures." The two decades from 1920 to 1940, he continued (1945: 3), "stand out as years of remarkable progress in the technique of administration" unbalanced by equally noteworthy achievements in the conduct of legislative business (1945: 4). Whereas in 1945 the executive branch of government in America had adopted a wide number of extremely helpful organization and management improvements, most legislative bodies still lacked "effective organization for the discharge of their duties" (1945: 11). In substance, White went on to say, organization of America's legislatures is "about the same as it was a century ago." Our governmental system is out of balance, he observed, and increasing strains may be feared unless the policy-forming branch of government "can be lifted to a higher level of performance" (1945: 4). Another distinguished public administration expert, Marshall E. Dimock (1945: 24), said the problem confronting students of public administration in 1945 "is how to inculcate a greater respect for representative government in the holders of administrative power... and at the same time inject more administrative efficiency into popular assemblies."

While political scientists have not been as guilty as students of public administration in their neglect of legislative institutions, they have, as we noted above, greatly favored Congress as a subject of study over state legislatures. Moreover, as Eric Redman has noted (1973: 17), in their research on Congress they have viewed that body as an institution made up solely of the 535 men and women who are representatives and senators. In speaking of the role of the Senate staff, Redman notes (1973: 17) that in the postwar era it

> has grown to approximately 3,000 individuals—a fact the literature [of political science] rarely noted, and less often examined. It was as if the academic community had looked at the glamorous and highly visible tip of an iceberg and declared that tip to *be* the iceberg; the other 97 percent of the individuals who draw their pay from the Senate Disbursing Office, and who support that tip, were simply left in the murky depths.

Thus, we remain a long way from Willoughby's notion that public administration is a logical and relevant field within which to deal with the subject of legislatures and legislative improvement. Willoughby went on to argue (1934: 3) that "the primary objective of the study of government should be the determination of those principles and practices the adoption of which by governments will enable them most effectively, efficiently and economically to perform the functions assumed by, or imposed upon, them." The way to do this, he observed, was to approach "the study of government from what may be termed the problem standpoint; that is, of seeking to determine the nature of the problems which are presented to a people in creating and operating a machinery for the conduct of its political affairs." The student following this approach (1934: 3-4) "places himself, first, in the position of a constituent assembly having, as one of its first tasks, the determination of the provision that it shall make for the performance of the so-called legislative function; and, next, in the position of the legislative body itself in determining how it shall organize itself and what rules of procedure it shall adopt in order most efficiently to perform the duties entrusted to it."

Adopting the viewpoint of the actor in the situation as a person with purposes to be achieved, work to be done, and so forth, is clearly more compatible with those political scientists who specialize in public administration than with those who do not. Indeed, the non-"p.a." political scientists have prided themselves on taking the objective "observer" as opposed to "value-accepting participant" stance and have been extremely critical of the "p.a." types because of their orientation to "helping get the job done."

It could be argued that because the study of public administration is essentially a study of hierarchically arranged division-of-labor organizations, it is, therefore, inappropriate for the study of legislatures, which are non-hierarchically arranged bargaining systems. The accusation made by George Galloway (1953: 352) that "analysis of the internal power structure of Congress . . . reveals that it violates all the basic principles of public administration," conveys a judgment of condemnation. And Gene Poschman (1970: 185-186) has noted that the traditional image of social scientists of Congress was that of an institution "contaminated by politics, manipulated by pluralistic interest, held tightly by ties to the local community, and generally devoid of the rationalizing characteristics of proper organization." It is certainly true that public administration began as a field with hierarchically arranged organizations in mind. However, during the past forty years, and particularly since World War II, the study of public administration has adopted a number of organizational models in addition to the hierarchically arranged structure. One of these is the "decision-making" model, in which an organization is viewed as a shaper of the premises of decisions. Another model, which might be termed "the economic," views organizations as situations for exchange of information and rewards based on a concept of a market. Our purpose here is not to review the various organizational models currently in vogue with students of public administration; rather, we simply wish to dispel the notion that the study of public administration utilizes only the hierarchically arranged model of organization.

Since 1945 many improvements have been introduced into American legislatures, particularly since 1964 when the U.S. Supreme Court decision in *Reynolds v. Sims* required all state legislatures to reapportion on the principle of "one man, one vote," thus ending rural control of state legislatures. Substantial effort is now being devoted to the reform of state legislatures. Although evidence is lacking, nearly everyone involved in reform efforts agrees what the problems are and what should be done to solve them [1]: legislatures maintain too many standing committees, therefore committees should be consolidated; compensation is too low to attract able men, therefore salaries should be increased; legislatures do not meet often enough to do their jobs, therefore they should convene annually and have longer sessions. If there is one type of problem and one type of solution on which agreement by reformers is virtually unanimous, it is professional staffing.[2] According to the Advisory Commission on Intergovernmental Relations (1967: 243): "One of the most critical factors conditionirg the capacity of legislative leaders, committees, and individual members to respond to their growing responsibilities is staff." Without staff, the reform argument goes, legislators cannot possibly arrive at competent judgments, independent of governors, bureaucracies, and interest groups. They need greater assistance in gathering, processing, and assessing information. As Duane Lockhard (1966: 114) states, there is no satisfactory alternative, for "by not providing desperately needed help the legislature is assuredly undermining its own foundation."

Yet the recommendation for increased professional staffs, like other aspects of legislative reform, has been made before political scientists have produced descriptive and analytical accounts of the staff which legislatures already employ. Ralph K. Huitt (1964: 8), in a discussion of Congress that is relevant to state legislatures as well, made a persuasive argument that the low level of knowledge about how legislatures work impedes the effectiveness of suggestions for change: "What we lack is a solid base of research which would make possible educated guesses as to who would be served by what kinds of changes and what the costs would be."

Ten years ago in a review of the literature on legislative behavior, Norman Meller (1965: 777) stated: "Staffing as a factor in the shaping of legislative product and the facilitating of legislative action remains almost wholly unresearched." Even today, little is known about this aspect of the legislative process, and there is a pressing need for more systematic and intensive studies of legislative improvement. Indeed, a review of the current state of actual knowledge concerning the role of professional staff and their effects upon legislative operations is an unrewarding task, for knowledge of this kind is impressively slight.

It is our contention that current approaches to the study of legislative modernization and improvement provide a highly inhibiting framework for research and theory construction. There are two important aspects that we propose to discuss: (1) conventional assumptions of the relationship of professional staffs to legislative bodies must be reviewed, with an emphasis on the empirical soundness of current theories, e.g., the one-sided view of the policy role legislative aides do play; and (2) certain aspects of organization theory suggest themselves as means of understanding the role of the staff and may offer some new insights into legislative structures and their environments.

PROFESSIONAL STAFFING AND CONVENTIONAL WISDOM

As we stated earlier, it has been the contention of many political scientists studying legislatures, and often of reformers within the legislature itself, that increases in staff expertise and a general upgrading of information resources are necessary if legislatures are to retain or regain their law-making capacities and to escape complete dominance by the executive.[3] At the same time, it is often stressed that staff appointments based on patronage and political considerations are ill suited to modern needs. What is preferable, according to this view, is a competent "professional" staff for the legislature—a staff well versed in the subject matter, accessible to, and capable of, augmenting the capacity of each member to make rational policy choices.

A great deal depends on how one defines "professionalism" in this context. "Professionalism" has been generally used (Kaufman, 1956: 1060) to indicate not merely competence but "neutral competence" as well—performance "according to explicit, objective standards rather than ... personal or party or other obligations and loyalties." This presumes the existence of independent fact, absolute and accepted, or waiting to be discovered. If fact cannot be demonstrated, then opinion is to be arrived at objectively and impersonally so as to approximate the detached character of fact. This is no more than a reflection of the dichotomy between fact and value—the former, external, the latter, personal—which troubles the social sciences.

Public administration once adopted this dichotomy between fact and value judgment by purporting to separate administration from politics.[4] In theory the administrator, as the expert, was to apply externally determined policy in accordance with scientific principles of management. Active participation in shaping these policies was suspect, for this would introduce subjective values. On the level of goals, in his capacity as administrator he could conscientiously enter only into development of objective professional standards and administrative techniques. The formation and declaration of public policy were to be functions of politics, not of administration.

Legislative service agencies were established and multiplied while this concept of public administration flourished (See Meller, 1967: 382). They were staffed by men who helped to elaborate this theory of public administration, as well as by those whose education was molded by it.[5] The impartiality of the administrator was matched in the legislative sphere by a similar professional standard for the guidance of the legislative service aide. In addition, the legislative service agency's concern with governmental matters about which an objective, nonevaluative approach was the rule when considered by the public administrator, also encouraged similarity of methodology. Staffing is to the organizational image of the legislature "what city managers are to the organizational image of local government, what responsible parties are for American politics, what school administrators are to local school boards" (Poschman, 1970: 226).

Today, public administration recognizes the decision-making role of the administrator.[6] To a greater or lesser degree, depending upon his place in the hierarchy,[7] the administrator may now properly participate in policy-making which involves not only judgments but also action based on them. Those advocating increased professional staffing for legislatures, however, generally continue to advocate scientific detachment from values and deny that staff takes any part in the actual shaping of policy, claiming their aloofness from value controversies.[8] Thus, many of the recommendations for increased legislative staffing, while they point to and promise to alleviate certain problems encountered by legislators in a day of complex policy decisions and executive-bureaucratic ascendance, reflect what seems to be a one-sided view of the policy role legislative staff aides do play. They suggest that experts do or should operate in a political vacuum. It is as if to say "that politics and partisanship are but unfortunate harbingers of a corrupt yesterday; and that good government, clean government, efficient government must come from the experts."[9]

Such recommendations and normative statements regarding the "proper role" of professional staffs of legislatures need to be grounded on empirical evidence. The only adequate test of the relative validity of the many diverse ideas on legislative staffing is how they have worked in practice. Since a number of state legislatures now have been operating with a sizable professional staff for some time, it might be desirable to examine the nature and workings of one of these staffs. This is what this study proposes to do with an examination of the work and functions of professional staffs in the New York State Legislature.[10] The discussion will center around four staff capabilities suggested by Samuel C. Patterson (1970)—intelligence, integration, innovation, and influence. Although these functions overlap, each is of sufficient importance to warrant separate consideration.

THE FUNCTIONS OF THE STAFF

INTELLIGENCE

One of the visible capabilities of the staff involves the intelligence function of the legislature.[11] The whole legislative procedure "is built around the process of acquiring information and intelligence with respect to particular conditions and situations, and the application of that information to the fashioning of laws."[12] Information provides the premises for decision or action. By one definition (Forrester, 1962: 37-38), decision-making is simply "the process of converting information into action." Policy or decision rules guide the decision-maker in relating information sources to resulting decision flows. A number of typologies of the decision-making process have been suggested. We shall utilize Herbert Simon's (1965: 53-56) definition of a three-phase decision process: finding occasions for making decisions (intelligence activity); finding possible courses of action (design activity); and choosing among possible courses of action (choice activity). Information—intelligence, news, facts, data—is essential to all phases of the process. The political decision-maker needs two types of information: "technical knowledge that defines the content of a policy issue; and political knowledge of the relative strength of competing claims and of the consequences of alternative decisions on a policy issue."[13] It is a common assumption that "bad" or "wrong" decisions in politics as in business stem from insufficient or improperly processed information,[14] and increased legislative staffs are often justified on the basis of providing more complete and accurate information.[15]

Research on Congress (Hattery and Hofheimer, 1954; Kovenock, 1964) has found that the legislative staff is a major source of information, and recent research on the New York State Legislature (Jennings and Milstein, 1970) resulted in similar findings.

Staffers are "facts-and-figures" men, and they spend a great deal of their working time engaged in processing information and supplying it to legislators. Ninety-seven percent of the staff members interviewed, in describing their activities, mentioned information-gathering or obtaining intelligence as one of their functions[16] (see Table 1). As one staff man said:

TABLE 1
INTELLIGENCE FUNCTION PERCEIVED BY LEGISLATIVE STAFF MEMBERS*

Activity	Proportion of Staffers Naming Each Activity in		
	Finance Committees' Staffs	Central Staff	Leadership Staffs
Planning and Conducting Hearings: selecting witnesses; notifying interested groups and executive agencies; setting room and time; balancing witnesses; preparing questions; briefing legislators; writing summaries.	80%	80%	47%
Bill Drafting: drafting bills; drafting amendments; preparing memoranda to accompany bills; writing committee reports.	73	100	88
Participation in Executive Sessions: attending executive sessions to explain bill or report; to draft amendments; marking up bill; discuss technical provisions; point up policy questions; keep track of decisions.	97	67	88
Preparing for and Assisting During Floor Action: draft bill manager's opening statement; preparing memoranda to use on floor; sit with legislator and aid him; aiding other legislators	83	40	47
Oversight of Administration: conferences with top departmental officials; investigation; handling casework; examining agency reports; reviewing administrative actions and changes in advance.	43	87	24

*Percentages total more than 100 since most respondents named more than one activity.

> The main job of the staff is to feed members relevant information. We are a continuous body of knowledge renewing the legislature. The members are too busy to become experts in the many areas they have to deal in. Oh, they're aware of the broad panorama, but I have the luxury of being able to examine certain issues in detail. I look at five or ten questions and I have all year to examine them. The legislators must look at thousands during the course of the session. The staff is the main resource enabling the legislator to get in-depth information on his problem.

Legislators also noted the staff as a major source of information, as Table 2 indicates. An astute staff member of the Senate Finance Committee summed up the job of the staff man:

> We are finders of facts. We are assemblers and analyzers of facts. What the legislators are looking for are not experts in the dozens of fields represented by the executive agencies. Rather they feel they need persons of broad education and experience capable of doing factual reports which correlate data from government publications, committee reports, the statutes, statistical abstracts, reports of executive departments, periodicals, newspapers, professional and trade associations. In other words, they want people competent enough to turn to quickly for particular statistics and data and to analyze and review those data from the viewpoint of the legislative branch.

An examination of the work staff members do in planning and conducting hearings, bill drafting, preparing committee reports and bill memo-

TABLE 2
SOURCES OF INFORMATION FOR STUDYING THE FACTS ABOUT BILLS

Sources	Percentage of Responding Legislators Noting Source (n=51)
Legislative staff	72
Interest groups	24
Sponsor and memorandum	20
Executive agencies	16
Counsels, committee reports	14
Centralized legislative research agencies (OLR, Legislative Reference Library, etc.)	6
The leadership	4
Mass media	2
Other members	2

randa, participating in executive sessions, and preparing for and assisting during floor action will reveal the degree to which the staff participates in the legislative process.

One of the most extensive sources of information for the legislature consists of legislative hearings relative to specific problems and legislative proposals.[17] It is the function of the staff to plan and conduct these hearings.

Planning and Conducting Hearings

Selection of Witnesses Seventy-five percent of the legislators interviewed and 71% of the staffers stated that the staff usually selected the witnesses for hearings. Occasionally, legislators would provide the staff with the names of individuals whom they (the legislators) wished to have testify on particular subjects. Making up the roster of witnesses was, in most instances, a routine task. The selection of witnesses from the executive branch was left also entirely to the discretion of the agencies concerned. After a committee had announced in the newspaper that hearings would be held on a certain subject, representatives of organized groups and other interested parties generally took the initiative in requesting an opportunity to testify. Securing witnesses then consisted merely of notifying such individuals when they could appear.

Once in a while, on controversial measures where many more persons asked to testify than could be accommodated in the time available, the staff had the responsibility of protecting the committee against the charge of stacking the hearings. In such a situation, the professional staff would carefully check the tentative roster of witnesses to ensure that spokesmen for all the major viewpoints were included and that a rough balance between the pros and cons was maintained. On the other issues, where the staff had an active interest, their role was a more active one. As one staff man put it:

> I initially came to [staff organization] to work on Indian affairs. The Indian issue was one that had gained prominence in the media, it appeared something was wrong there, and that was my incentive to work here. We were able to convince the chairman to hold hearings on the issue. We brought in a number of Indians and bank representatives to testify about the housing shortage on the reservations. Since the tribe owns the land, the banks can't foreclose on the mortgage and are reluctant to lend money. We were able to find some sympathetic bank representatives and got a bill on the matter out of committee.

Preparation of Questions Sixty-six percent of the staffers said that they customarily prepared lists of questions for the members to ask in the hearings. These ranged from a general statement of problem areas on which additional information was required to an integrated set of precisely formulated questions typed on index cards. In addition, most of the legislative aides wrote out questions that occurred to them during hearings and passed them to the chairman or to other committee members especially interested in the area being discussed.

Briefing Committee Members Practices among legislative aides in supplementing written staff materials with oral explanations of subjects of committee action varied widely. In most instances, briefings before a hearing were given on an individual basis and were usually confined to the chairman. But nearly all the professional staffs willingly extended that service to other committee members on request. These individual briefings ran the gamut from a hurried attempt five minutes before the start of a hearing to acquaint the chairman with a list of questions prepared for him to going over a bill in detail with him for a whole afternoon or evening.

Bill Drafting

Forty percent of the staffers and 37% of the legislators stated that staff members usually drafted at least some bills and amendments.

The drafting of a bill normally is thought of as merely framing in clear and unambiguous language the results of a decision previously made. Technically, the draftsman is supposed to be concerned only with the formal requirements of constitutionality, not with substantive matters which go to the heart of the proposal. Yet staff members who were engaged in bill drafting stated that they brought every foreseeable problem to the attention of the legislator. Usually, the legislators would then discuss with them the risk of successful judicial challenges and the legal feasibility of alternative approaches. One assemblyman described the situation as follows:

> Occasionally when I propose a bill and ask the staff to draft it for me, they'll come back and say, "There's a problem here," or "We can't do it this way." Often they're able to point out what we can do to achieve the purpose of the proposal without risking it being thrown out by the courts.

When one adds to the situation of clear unconstitutionality the more numerous ones where legality is only doubtful, the position of the staffer drafting legislation no longer appears so remote from the decision process.

The staff man helps to identify possible alternatives and to make the final selection.

When the final decision has been made, those staff members drafting legislation materially contribute to the shaping of minor elements of policy. Except for the simplest of amendatory bills, the staffer proceeds unobtrusively to add the flesh of details to the outline of general principles provided by the requestor. Of course, the staffer must operate within certain guidelines and the draft finally adopted must meet with the approval of the legislator, but ratification of a submitted proposal is quite different from accepting delivery of a mere rephrasing of minute directions. The staff man attempts to embody the spirit of the proposal into the draft of the law, and usually obtains instructions from the requestor concerning those features which might prove controversial. One member of Assembly Central Staff described the process:

> [Name of Assemblyman] had a proposal regarding the workmen's compensation laws. Together we worked out a bill. I checked with him to see whether he wanted the existing agency to have the responsibility for enforcing the proposed statute or whether he felt we should seek to create a new executive agency. He felt that we should stay with the existing agency. But the question of which department within that agency would be the most appropriate to undertake the regulation was left to me to decide. I chose to specify the proper department rather than drawing up the bill so that the head of the agency was empowered to assign the function as he saw fit.

As a legislator noted, "Even intelligent observers often gloss over the fact that the contents of a legislative proposal are not inevitable, but that the staff man drafting it suggests the details of the tentative bill. Often, it is only later that these 'administrative details' and 'subsidiary concerns' become apparent and their importance recognized."

Preparing Memoranda To Accompany Bills The memorandum to accompany a bill is a very important document of advocacy and interpretation. Its primary purpose is to afford the members of the legislature sufficient information to evaluate the measure intelligently. Members of the legislature not on the committee considering a piece of legislation rely on the memorandum accompanying the bill for their knowledge of it (see Table 2).

Ninety-six percent of the legislators and 84% of the staff members surveyed stated that the memoranda to accompany bills were a staff product. On a major measure, the memorandum occasionally became a lengthy report on which the staff collaborated.

Before starting to do a report or memorandum, the staff usually consulted the chairman on what to emphasize in it. But for the most part, the staff drafted the memoranda on bills without much direct supervision from the committee.

Assembly Central Staff, in an attempt to be nonpartisan, has sought to improve the objectivity of its memoranda by utilizing a number of mechanical devices. For example, emotion-laden words are removed, comprehensiveness of presentation is required, and quotations from others are included.

The motivation underlying this cautious approach is the desire to establish Central Staff as a permanent legislative research arm. Two members of Central Staff discussed this attempt to be objective and nonpartisan:

> I try to be as objective as possible in my report, analyzing all the alternatives, presenting the pros and cons, and listing the groups for and against the proposal. But once you're here for a while and you earn the chairman's trust, he'll say "What do you think? How do you weigh it?" So you tell him. And you tell him what it means for his district and what it means for him politically.

> Most of our work involves quick information retrieval, briefing of bills, and administrative work, like setting up hearings, making out agendas, and turning out press releases. Much of your impact depends on whether or not you develop a personal relationship with the chairman. Then, you often find yourself doing work that is not outlined by the director [of Central Staff] when you get the job. You're asked for advice on strategy, on whether to introduce two similar bills at the same time or bring them up for debate separately, on tactics.

All these legislative staff members operate, then, within the broad political context of the jurisdictions they serve. Lack of time and the need to play a significant role compel the weeding out or the playing down of the too-theoretical, the politically impractical. This is not to suggest that research topics and staff work are determined by partisan political consideration, but that the choice of content and detail of treatment cannot help being influenced by the use to which data may be put. Usually the staffer is acutely aware of this orientation only in situations involving politically explosive issues where obvious efforts toward impartiality and comprehensiveness of scope must be displayed. The situation of the staffer was described by one aide as follows:

> I try to be realistic in terms of the framework I'm working in. You can't be effective here without being political. In some cases, the

political is the single most important consideration. If I don't take into account the political considerations, I'll have no influence at all. If I'm examining the alternatives to a problem, I have to examine the political. You wouldn't be doing your job if you weren't aware of the political situation and didn't take it into account. After all, all these men [the legislators] are political animals and you have to understand that. I don't let political considerations bias my research, but I don't ignore them either. I have to do so to gain the respect and trust of the committee chairmen.

Participation in Executive Sessions

Eighty-seven percent of the staffers and 78% of the legislators stated that staff members usually attended executive sessions at which a bill, report, or other item on which they had worked was under consideration. There the staff man rendered a variety of services, ranging from acting as a reading clerk to drafting amendments. But for the most part, he was available to furnish additional information and explanation of whatever project he was handling. When a bill was being marked up, he would discuss technical provisions, point up policy questions, analyze proposed changes, keep track of committee decisions, and incorporate them in successive revisions of the bill.

Preparing for and Assisting During Floor Action

Sixty-three percent of the staff members and 41% of the legislators, in describing the work of the staff, mentioned their activities in preparing for and assisting during floor action. Before a major bill came up for consideration, staff members stated that they took several preparatory steps. In both chambers, the staff nearly always drafted the statement with which the chairman (or other manager) opened the debate on a bill. Customarily, this introductory speech summarized the entire measure and set forth the committee's position on any controversial aspects of it.

One legislator noted, "The legislator tells the staff man what he wants to say, but the tone and language are the staffer's." Frequently, the staff would make up a series of brief memoranda containing answers to certain arguments and questions that probably would be raised. Then when one of them came up, the staff could simply encircle the relevant portion of the "prefabricated" reply and hand it to the chairman to read off in rejoinder. Generally, the staff assembled a file of reference materials for use during the floor action of the bill.

Usually, the professional aide who had done the bulk of the staff work on the bill accompanied the chairman on the floor. There he assisted the chairman in many ways: locating the references for him, obtaining additional information, analyzing proposals and arguments advanced there, and suggesting responses to them. Also, sometimes he reworked amendments offered there to make them acceptable to the committee or relayed the chairman's direction on that score to the legislative counsel, who often was present in the rear of the chamber.

Oversight of Administration

The New York State Legislature exercises oversight of the administrative establishment in a number of different ways. Among these are conferences with top departmental officials; investigation; handling casework; requiring periodic reports on the status of particular programs; and reviewing or passing upon discrete administrative actions in advance. Members of the professional staff were important participants in these operations, according to 48% of the staff members and 35% of the legislators.

For example, the periodic reports prepared by executive agencies were filed and utilized by the legislative staffs as reference works. Occasionally, professional aides prepared summaries of them for the members of their committees. Once in a while, such reports or excerpts from them were included in committee reports—generally as appendices.

Executive line agencies are required by statute to submit to the legislature all administrative regulations (new rules or changes) thirty days before they are to take effect. The review by the legislature of these regulations is exercised mainly through the staffs. Although the staff has no formal power to disallow such rules, two high-ranking employees of the Division of the Budget said that a new regulation or rule change to which the staff of the legislature objected was not likely to take effect until the point of disagreement was resolved. Said one Education Department official: "If the legislative committee staff doesn't like our proposal, we'll have rough sledding." A deputy commissioner in the Transportation Department added, "We never work up an important measure without consulting the legislative committee staff for its ideas and reactions."

Summary

The professional staffers see their role (and are seen) as performing an important "intelligence" (information-gathering) function for the legislative system. Staffs investigate, research, schedule, edit, compile, and distribute much of the information on which legislative decisions are based. The staff network is the only organization with sole responsibility for directing and filtering the flow of information to the legislature.

In fact, as we will discuss in greater detail later, staffers are seen as being important, in part, because of the strategic place they occupy in the flow of information in the legislative system. The legislature can be viewed organizationally (Froman, 1968), and an organization, by its very definition, implies and "requires the introduction of constraints and restrictions to reduce diffuse and random communications to channels appropriate for the accomplishment of organizational objectives" (Katz and Kahn, 1966: 225). A network of human communicators introduces some immediate inefficiencies to organizational decision-making, such as distortion, errors in transmission, resources absorbed in internal communication, and short-run communications overload (Downs, 1967: 178). Hierarchy and specialization introduce more serious problems to information processing. Hierarchy is conducive to "concealment and misrepresentation" in systems where subordinates are upwardly mobile or advocates of subprograms (Downs, 1967: 116-118). Specialization intensifies blockage and distortion. Katz and Kahn (1966: 228) conclude that the most general limitation to information coding and processing in human organization is that "the position people occupy in organizational space will determine their perception and interpretation of incoming information and their search for additional information."

One critical problem in organizational communication is the strong tendency to overload certain decision-makers with information. Individuals working under conditions of information overload have exhibited a number of often maladaptive reactions: (1) omission—failing to process some of the information; (2) error—processing information incorrectly; (3) queuing—delaying during periods of peak load in the hope of catching up later; (4) filtering—neglecting to process certain types of information according to predetermined priorities; (5) approximation—eliminating categories of discrimination (a blanket and imprecise way of responding); (6) employing multiple channels, as in decentralization; and (7) escape from the task.[18] In the specific case of communications from constituents, Lewis Anthony Dexter (Bauer, Pool, and Dexter, 1963) found that congressmen had developed a number of similar techniques for coping with overload.[19] In New York, it seems that the legislator, overloaded with messages, reports, memoranda, and so on, turns the processing of information over to his staff assistants. The staffers can allow information which supports their personal preferences to pass on to the legislators and cull out that which opposes their preferences.

INTEGRATION

Integration is the degree to which there is a working together or a meshing together or mutual support among legislative staff subgroups. It can be defined as the degree to which the staff is able to minimize conflict among its subgroups by heading off or resolving the conflicts that arise. A necessary condition for integration is the existence of a fairly consistent set of norms, widely followed by the staff members. Another necessary condition for integration is the existence of control mechanisms (i.e., socializing and sanctioning mechanisms) capable of maintaining reasonable conformity to norms.[20] In another study, one of the authors (Balutis: 1973) has discussed the consensus that exists among staff members concerning their perceived behavioral norms. Therefore, in this article we will examine the degree of interrelationship or interaction between various legislative staff subgroups[21] and between legislative staffers and other groups (see Table 3).

Legislative staffs contribute to the integration of committees, they contribute to intercameral integration, and they contribute to legislative-executive integration. Starting from a base of loyalty to the committee or leader they serve, the staffs build their own internal esprit and sense of

TABLE 3
CONTACTS NAMED BY STAFFERS*

Contact	Proportion on Staffers Naming Each Contact in		
	Finance Committee Staffs (n=30)	Central Staff (n=15)	Leadership Staffs (n=17)
Governor's staff	23%	67%	82%
Executive agency staffs	90	100	30
Division of the Budget	57	7	—
Interest groups	70	60	35
Staff counterparts in other chamber	67	33	24
Staff of other committees in same chamber	33	47	35
Rank-and-file	7	27	30
Leadership	17	13	82
Miscellaneous (OLR, Legislative Reference, Bill Drafting Commission)	7	7	6

*Percentages total more than 100 since most respondents named more than one contact.

identification. Seventy-one percent of the staff members interviewed stated that their groups were tightly knit, worked closely together, and were frequently close socially. The manner in which close working harmony is lubricated by informal ties was described by a Senate aide in this way:

> There's a lot of interchange, interaction, contacts back and forth on the staff. We help each other out and discuss any problems we have and the projects we're working on with each other. We try to coordinate our work and our approach across bills . . . we're small and we can work together easily. We have coffee together in the morning, eat together, play handball and squash with each other, and party together.

Negatively, the highly integrated staffs eliminate a possible source of internal disruption. The fact that staff members are not dissatisfied with their work and are not engaged in squabblings and disagreements removes a barrier to interaction. But it seems likely, as well, that by their efforts they increase the degree of harmony among the legislators for whom they work.

An examination of staff interrelationships will reveal the degree to which they contribute to intracameral and intercameral integration.

Interstaff Relations in the Same Chamber

Relations among legislative staffs in the same house were described by staff members as being infrequent, informal, and characterized by cooperation rather than collaboration. The main dealings occurred between legislative committee aides and the staffs of the finance committees[22] and committee personnel and leadership staffers assigned to "monitor" committee legislation.[23]

One member of the Assembly Central Staff described their relationship with the staff of Ways and Means in this way:

> We have extensive contacts with the staff of Ways and Means. Policy and fiscal considerations are so inextricably interwoven that we have to be in touch with each other. They're so much more knowledgeable in fiscal affairs than we are that we turn to them for their expertise. The same holds true because of our knowledge of substantive policy matters; they come to us. They sometimes utilize our reports and hearings. We're automatically drawn to each other as reciprocal sources of information.[24]

Relations among the staff of legislative committees in the same house were usually confined to situations in which there were jurisdictional overlaps. In such cases, they discussed only matters of mutual interest. Occasionally, they procured from one another analyses of bills, staff studies, or other unpublished materials that had already been prepared. However, committee staffs rarely collaborated with each other or with leadership staffs in the preparation of memoranda, reports, or legislation.

Staffers mentioned several factors responsible for this lack of collaboration among staffs intracamerally, as Table 4 indicates. The most frequently mentioned was the heavy workload. Aides stated that they just did not have the time to attend the hearings and executive sessions of other committees or to assist their staffs in the preparation of bills and reports. Also mentioned was the short deadline under which the members of the staff frequently operated. This prevented them from submitting reports or bills to other legislative aides for review of the portions impinging upon the latter's sphere. Finally, as a general rule, collaboration among the staffs could not greatly exceed that among their respective committees or legislators. Thus, staff collaboration depended on the personal compatibilities (or lack thereof) of key legislators.

Interstaff Relations Between the Two Houses

As with interstaff contact in the same chamber, relations between corresponding staff in the two chambers were described as being predominantly sporadic, informal, and cooperative rather than collaborative in nature. The majority staffs of the finance committees, for example, sought to avoid any contact during the period when the budget was before the legislature "in order to arrive at an independent analysis."[25] When the legislature was not in session, however, the members of the staffs would

TABLE 4
REASONS GIVEN BY STAFFERS FOR LACK OF COLLABORATION IN SAME CHAMBER*

Reason	Proportion of Staffers Naming Reason (n=42)
Heavy workload	62%
Short deadline	40
Lack of collaboration among legislators	33

*Percentages total more than 100 since most respondents named more than one reason.

often combine their trips to the field to study agency operations. Since the staffs for the minority on the finance committees were smaller in number, they made an effort to work together on budget analysis. As one minority aide said, "What we try to do is parcel out the work among ourselves so that we can better analyze the entire budget. Instead of each staff in each house handling eight to ten agencies, we divide up the agencies and departments so that each analyst is handling only four to five."

Conversations—principally over the telephone—constituted the bulk of the dealings between the staffs in the two chambers. Several maintained a fairly systematic interchange of information. But most of them contacted each other only irregularly in connection with a specific matter of mutual interest.

Collaboration is most clearly manifested when the two houses pass different versions of a bill and the differences have to be resolved. Sometimes the staff will meet prior to meetings between the committee chairmen involved or the leadership to identify areas of real agreement and disagreement between Assembly and Senate members. More often, the legislators themselves do not actually meet, but rather the differences are resolved by the relevant Assembly and Senate staff personnel. A staff aide to then Senate Majority Leader Earl Brydges described an episode of this kind in discussing his relations with his Assembly staff counterpart:

> [Assembly staff member] and I have worked out some tough problems in conference together. The New York City school decentralization bill two years ago is a case in point. The leadership more or less gave a blank check to the staff to resolve the issue. Together with [Assembly staff member], I came up with a workable plan. It certainly wasn't perfect, but it was the best possible under the circumstances. We got our respective leaders to agree, and the bill passed both houses. Here the bill was more a staff product than a legislators' product.

The lack of collaboration on reports or legislation was attributed by staff members to a number of obstacles to joint undertaking by Senate and Assembly staffs (see Table 5). One of the most fundamental was the difference in the timetables of the two chambers. Several weeks often elapsed between the consideration of the same measure by the Assembly and the Senate. It would have been difficult for the staff in the house not handling the matter until later to spare the time for a joint study of it when the other house first took it up. Since the legislators, not their staffs, decided the order of business, it was not possible for the latter to integrate their work to any great extent.

TABLE 5
REASONS GIVEN BY STAFFERS FOR LACK OF COLLABORATION WITH OTHER HOUSE*

Reason	Proportion of Staffers Naming Reason (n=42)
Different schedules	45%
Committee and institutional rivalry	74
Heavy workload	38
Personal differences	55

*Percentages total more than 100 since most respondents named more than one reason.

As in the case of intracameral staff relations, corresponding staffs in the Assembly and Senate, because of their small size and heavy workloads, did not have time very often to attend the hearings and executive sessions of each other's committees or to engage in joint projects. In a few instances, a marked differential in the competence of the two staffs further deterred them from seeking each other's help. Interacting with all these elements were the personalities of the individuals concerned. In several cases there was considerable incompatibility—if not downright enmity—between opposite numbers on the staffs of Senate and Assembly committees.

Finally, as was true intracamerally, the relations between the corresponding Senate and Assembly committees or leadership largely determined the collaboration possible between their staffs. And the parallel committees in the two houses evinced little inclination toward joint action. Once more, there were numerous impediments such as the inertia of custom and precedent and the institutional rivalries, jealous regard for independence and prerogatives, and differences in perspective and procedures of both the committees and their parent chambers.

With the Executive Branch

It is accepted by now that although constitutions separate authority among the three branches of government, there is a good deal of overlap among the institutions and that, in fact, they share power and responsibility for legislation. To date, however, there have been relatively few empirical studies of how the branches bridge the formal separation and interact with each other; there are even fewer studies of arrangements between individual legislative committees and related executive agencies.[26]

One bridge between the branches is through the professional staffs of the legislature and their counterparts in the executive agencies and in the governor's office. Members of the governor's staff, executive agency staffs, and Division of the Budget personnel were named most often by legislative staffers as contacts (see Table 3). Legislative staffs thus facilitate legislative-executive integration through their close relations with executive personnel—with commissioners and assistant commissioners, agency heads, department chiefs, general counsels, program analysts, members of the governor's staff, and budget and fiscal staff. The interaction between the staff was described on one aide:

> Last year, [a Senator] contacted us about developing what turned out to be the Administrative Procedures Act. The Governor's office worked with us on it along with some people from [several executive agencies], and we became very dependent on each other. In other words, neither side controlled the development of the bill one way or the other—there was a balance. We were able to overcome the objections that had led the Governor to veto a similar bill the year before and to turn out a solid piece of legislation.

Staff members noted a variety of purposes for interacting with the executive branch, as Table 6 shows.

One of the most valuable—certainly the most heavily in demand—of the numerous services departmental staffs afforded the legislative aides was the provision of information of various sorts. With their immense and well-equipped staffs, including field forces distributed throughout the state, collecting statistics and other intelligence, the administrative agencies had amassed a vast reservoir of data that the legislative staffs could never have

TABLE 6
REASONS GIVEN BY STAFFERS FOR CONTACTING EXECUTIVE BRANCH*

Reason	Proportion of Staffers Naming Reason (n=52)
Exchange of information	90%
In preparing staff studies	82
In analyzing bills	44
In bill drafting	27
On memoranda and reports to accompany bills	95
In organizing and conducting hearings	16
For help during floor action	11

*Percentages total more than 100 since most respondents named more than one reason.

hoped to duplicate. Legislative aides stated that had they been unable to obtain information in the possession of the executive branch, they could not have functioned successfully. Although sometimes legislative staffs obtained supplementary factual materials from interest groups, private research institutes, and other organizations, the executive branch was their primary source of data.

Reciprocally, agency personnel frequently sought the advice of legislative staffs—mainly concerning the attitudes and preferences of legislative leaders and key legislators and what the legislature was likely to accept or reject. Usually, legislative aides and departmental personnel obtained information from and consulted each other on an ad hoc basis.

Legislative aides had little difficulty obtaining access to information with which to evaluate or challenge the executive's programs. Naturally, an agency would not volunteer information on the shortcomings of its proposals. But 94% of the staffers interviewed said that, when asked a specific question, the departments would nearly always supply the information sought even though it might be adverse to bills sponsored by them, reflected on their administration, or was detrimental in other respects. Although an agency might include supplementary explanatory material to present its response in the most favorable light, it ordinarily would furnish the data requested, no matter how deleterious. To have done otherwise would have jeopardized its long-run interest in maintaining cordial relations with the legislature and its staff.

Therefore, if the departments made any omission in their presentations to the legislature whether inadvertently or intentionally, the main problem posed for its staff was to detect those gaps and to ask for the data to fill them rather than to develop substitute sources of such information.[27] Sometimes the staff man could call on personal acquaintances in the executive branch whom he could trust not to reveal his requests for help. As one Senate Finance Committee aide put it, "No matter what administration is in office, there's always someone in there who thinks everything is wrong and is willing to tell you about it."

At certain times, information-gathering served merely as a guise. Members of the staff were called upon occasionally to obtain material when all concerned appreciated that a factual report would add little significant knowledge and that the staff was functioning as a legislative prod. Instead of personally attempting to expedite or modify action by an executive department, the legislator addressed an inquiry for information to the staff, confident that when the department was contacted and queried, the latter would reappraise the course it was following as a precautionary measure, and do so without the legislator's identity having been disclosed.

Similarly, a staffer empowered to communicate with a department for background information preparatory to drawing up "corrective" legislation may be communicating legislative concern.

When preparing compilations of background information or other reports for the legislature, departmental personnel generally consulted the appropriate legislative staffs about the contents, emphases, and format. Reciprocally, legislative aides sometimes discussed the organization and content of their staff studies with executive branch personnel and frequently asked them to review those studies—especially any portions pertaining to agency operations and procedures—for errors of fact and occasionally of interpretation. Usually, they sought the advice and criticism of departmental experts on an individual basis.

Occasionally, when the Division of the Budget had been slow in clearing an agency report on a bill, a legislative aide would call the agency legal staff for an "advance opinion" on the measure. Very frequently when analyzing a departmental bill, a legislative staff member would contact the agency counsel who had drafted it to ascertain the policy and legal implications intended. And throughout the consideration of an administrative bill, legislative staffers often asked the agency legal staffs to evaluate the effects and practicality of proposed amendments.

Once in a while, during the formative stages of a major administrative measure, departmental counsel would seek suggestions from the legislative staffs concerned on the content, format, and other aspects of the proposed bill in order to increase its acceptability to members of the legislature. Also, in such cases, the agency legal staffs customarily submitted preliminary drafts of the bill to legislative staff members for criticism. Conversely, when a legislative aide had prepared amendments to a departmental measure, he ordinarily checked with the agency lawyers to ensure that the amendments accomplished what the legislature wanted. And for the drafting of amendments of a highly technical nature, a number of legislative staff members occasionally resorted to the departmental legal staffs in lieu of the Bill Drafting Commission or the committee legislative counsel. For where thousands of agency interpretations of laws and regulations, actuarial or other specialized skills, or extremely complicated administrative operations were involved, legislative legal experts would have had to refer to the agency staffs anyway. Hence, when the departments and the legislature had congenial views and especially where modifications in departmental bills were entailed, legislative aides often turned to the agency draftsman.

When engaged in a data-gathering task preparatory to drafting a bill, a staff man occasionally discovered that what the legislator wished to accomplish did not require additional legislative authorization, but could be achieved under some existing statute. If it was only an administrative imbroglio which had resulted in an impasse, or if inadequate administrative coordination was to blame for inaction, the staffer, after receiving the legislator's approval, endeavored to contact the administrative agencies involved in order to further the legislator's purpose. As one staff man put it, "In the course of mediating between a legislator and an agency, it's often very difficult not to take an active part in influencing the course of the final decision."

In this and a number of other ways the professional staff of the legislature occasionally has the opportunity to help bridge the gap between the legislative and executive departments. A full understanding of all the ramifications of the administrative problem may result in presenting a factual situation to the legislator in a more sympathetic light. A member of the staff of the Senate Finance Committee described one such case:

> Last year, [a Senator] wanted more done with narcotics education and he had this press release ready jumping up and down on the Education Department for not doing enough. He came to me and I agreed that more should be done. But there was a real question whether more could be done, so I arranged a meeting with a guy from Education. We went through it line by line, how many teachers are trained in this area, etc. Finally I asked him what difference it would make if we doubled the appropriation for this item. His answer was none, because there were just so many schools equipped to train people in this area and the legislature could appropriate $1,000,000 instead of $100,000 and it wouldn't make any difference for several years. In this case, [the Senator] was willing to listen and he saved himself some embarrassment. He could have started jumping up and down on the Education Department and they would have just said, "Look, . . ."

Similarly, the staff member can materially contribute to the amelioration of ruffled administrative feelings through the judicious outlining, at a propitious moment, of an offending legislator's position in a manner devoid of emotional involvement. One member of Assembly Central Staff discussed this area of this work:

> Every once in a while, one of the assemblymen will get four or five angry letters or phone calls from people back in the district and he'll start calling me and people in the agency and raising hell. We'll try to examine the problem and then go to the agency, be low-key, and explain the legislator's position and his perspective on the problem. After all, he's only trying to represent the people back home and get

reelected. Few of the agencies have thought through that element of their service that reaches the people; they're too concerned about what's going on in the central office. Often you can remind them of their other obligations.

With Interest Group Staffs

In his study of Washington lobbyists, Lester Milbrath found that lobbyists tended to spend only limited time with legislators and that they tended to spend more time with staff people. "In many instances," Milbrath (1963: 122) states, "such aides are very close to official decision-makers and participate significantly in their decision-making processes. . . . So useful are these aides, these brokers in communication, that many lobbyists say that in certain cases they prefer to confer with a trusted aide than with the decision-maker himself."

Interest groups constituted significant contacts for legislative staff members. Fifty-eight percent of the staffers mentioned interest groups as important points of contact and 90% of the interest group representatives surveyed stated that they had frequent contacts with legislative aides.

Most of the relations between legislative aides and the staffs of organized interest groups in their fields centered around the exchange of various kinds of information. The prevailing flow of information was from the interest groups to the legislative staffs. Most of that was volunteered by the interest group employees. But sometimes legislative staffers requested certain statistics or other information from them. "After all," said one Ways and Means Committee staffer, "the interest groups are the main collectors and repositories of technical information. If I want to know about union pension funds, who else would I go to other than the unions."

Generally, legislative staffs turned to interest groups for data not available elsewhere. But fairly often, legislative aides secured information from them as a check on that supplied by the executive branch. In this regard, a number of legislative staff members observed that their efficiency was considerably increased through the operations of interest group representatives. For the latter frequently pointed out shortcomings in the statements of administrative agencies or opposing interest groups which the legislative staffs might have overlooked and supplied detailed documentation for criticizing those statements.

Staff members utilize interest groups to check information supplied by other interest groups.

[Assembly Ways and Means Committee staff member] You have to be aware of the countervailing influence of the interest groups. . . .

An intelligent staffer can use the natural opposition within the lobbying community to gain valuable information.

Another staffer went on to state:

> Too much has been written about the evil interest of lobbyists. I've been here since 1963 and I've never been offered money by a lobbyist. I suppose it has happened, and happens, but legislators aren't bought by interest groups. It's not in the interest of lobbyists to lie to you. Their credibility is extremely important to them. They're not here just for one bill. They have a continued interest in legislation and they're not about to lie to you knowing they'll be back in the future for your help.

Interest group representatives in New York go where power is, or where they think power is, and the legislative staff is not shortchanged when it comes to contact with lobbyists. A lobbyist described the manner in which legislators use the staff to winnow proposals and how the staff, contacted first, can reverse the procedure and assist a lobbyist:

> The Speaker will say to me, "Go see Roberts [Albert Roberts, secretary of the Assembly Ways and Means Committee] and then let me read his report." If Roberts thinks there's no merit in the idea, the Speaker will usually drop it. If Roberts thinks the proposal has merit, the Speaker is likely to sponsor it or find someone to sponsor it.

A member of Assembly Central Staff added the following:

> I think we've come to be an intervening force between the legislators and interest groups. We still go to them for information because they continue to be valuable sources, but now we screen out some of the crap they try to give us. Where before, an interest group might call a legislator, now he'll tell them to come and see us first. We act as a filter for the legislature.

As was true throughout the entire area of interstaff relations, the dealings between the legislative aides and interest group employees were highly personalized. Undoubtedly, such relationships were influenced by the fact that a number of the legislative aides had previously been on the staffs of organized interest groups, were members of the interest groups, or were members of the same professional association as the interest group representatives.

Summary

The focus of this section has been on an examination of the relations between legislative staff members and other participants in the political subsystem—"significant others" within the legislature, in executive agencies, in the governor's office, and in various interest groups. Legislative staffers interact with members of the governor's staff, executive agency staffers, Budget personnel, interest group representatives, other staffers in the same chamber and in the other house, rank-and-file legislators, and the legislative leadership. These relationships provide much of the cement that holds the legislature together and binds the legislative and executive branches together. This network of staff interaction helps to establish lines of communication to and from the legislature through which staff members can obtain information and oversee administrative action. Personal friendships, previous work relationships, and membership in the same professional organizations are crucial elements in this network.

INNOVATION

Legislative staff members see themselves as having innovative capabilities (see Table 7). One of the reasons members of the legislative staff like their work is that they have the opportunity to innovate, to initiate public policy, or to see it initiated.

Several of the terms which have been used here have ambiguous meanings, and a discussion of two of them, "innovation" and "initiation," may serve a number of purposes. First, it will alert the reader to problems in the discussion that follows. And second, it may direct attention to the need for a more thorough discussion of these terms in the study of legislative decision-making.

TABLE 7
PROPORTION OF STAFFERS NAMING INNOVATION OR INITIATION AS FUNCTIONS

Staff	Proportion of Staffers Naming Functions (n=50)
Finance committees	53%
Central staff	67
Leadership staffs	29

Jack L. Walker (1969: 881) has defined an innovation "simply as a program or policy which is new to the states adopting it, no matter how old the program may be or how many other states have adopted it." What we are dealing with here is the process of adoption, not the process of invention or the creation of "new programs." Innovation, as defined by Walker (1969: 881) then, concentrates "on the way in which organizations select from proposed solutions the one most suited to their needs, and how the organizations come to hear about these new ideas in the first place."

Although the concept of "initiation" (or "initiative") has been used frequently by political scientists in describing policy-making, it has rarely, if ever, been specifically defined.[28] Harold Lasswell and Abraham Kaplan (1950) fail to mention the term "initiation" in their catalogue of political semantics, *Power and Society*. In the absence of specific definitions one must assume that standard dictionary usage is being followed. As often happens, however, dictionary definitions raise more questions than they answer. A typical definition of "initiative" is "the act of taking the first step or move"; it is the "responsibility for beginning or originating." It does not take much acquaintance with philosophy to see the nature of the futile journey on which this concept tempts one to begin. Perhaps a desire to avoid opening the Pandora's box of causation partly accounts for the dearth of specific definitions. Robert Dahl (1957: 203), for one, has explicitly stated his desire to steer clear of the host of problems connected with the concept of "cause."

Even if "initiation" were to be specifically defined, difficult questions would remain. Legislative proposals usually undergo modification between the time they are "initiated" and the time they are implemented. How much modification should the researcher allow before he begins to talk about "substitution" of a new proposal in lieu of the original?

In addition to the conceptual problems of studying "initiation," there are some empirical ones relating to practical difficulties of describing these phenomena. For example, just how is one to identify the initiator of a given proposal? Although Dahl seems to have little trouble identifying the initiators of policy proposals in New Haven, other political scientists cannot expect to be so fortunate.

Although this discussion has asked more questions than it has answered, hopefully it has served the two purposes previously mentioned. Innovation and initiation are somewhat slippery conceptions to be sure, but a number of staff people and legislators described projects which the staffers were undertaking at their own initiation, and many staffers described legislation which they themselves were working on.[29] As one experienced legislator noted, "Staff members, especially those with long tenure in key staff positions, are about as likely to initiate legislation as are legislators themselves. For example, Al Abrams, the secretary of the Senate, is the author of numerous pioneering laws, such as the Einstein and Schweitzer chairs founded by the legislature in the sciences and humanities."

Some staff members expressed a reluctance to play a too active role in initiating legislation. As one member of Central Staff put it:

> It's not part of our job here to sit around thinking up pieces of legislation and then to go to the assemblymen and tell them, "I think this is a good idea. I drew up this bill and I think you ought to introduce it." Sometimes, when you're examining a bill, you may find a problem in it, or a defect, and, in that case, we'd say, "You have a problem here and this is a way to take care of it," but whether the assemblyman does it or not is up to him. Sometimes if an assemblyman comes up with an idea for a bill, but it's just in a seminal stage, we'll work with him on it to make it a developed piece of legislation. But the idea comes from the legislator. We react to his ideas and suggestions.

A look at one of the legislative ideas that could claim Central Staff parentage points up the staff's role further and reveals the manner in which "professionalism" is linked to a role free of advocacy. In 1970, then-Assemblyman John Terry (R-Syracuse) began to develop a bill that would guarantee the public's right to scrutinize records of nearly all state and local governmental agencies. Terry dropped the so-called Freedom of Information Bill when he was elected to Congress later that year. Central Staff continued to refine the measure, and, in 1972, its sponsorship was taken over by Assemblyman Donald L. Taylor (R-Watertown) and Senator Ralph J. Marino (R-Long Island). The member of Central Staff who worked on the measure described his role:

> The "Freedom of Information Bill" wasn't a matter of the staff going to Terry and setting him on to the idea. I worked on the bill, but it was at Terry's direction. Our job here isn't to go around manipulating legislators like a bunch of puppets. We react to legislators' wishes, sentiments, etc. We don't get involved in politics, in working on matters from the district, etc. We're here to serve all the members of the Assembly, and if you start feeding ideas to one assemblyman or another, you get away from the ideal of being nonpartisan. It might get you into trouble.

Legislatively initiated projects like the "Freedom of Information Bill" displayed Central Staff ingenuity and revealed the importance of their skills to those assemblymen who sought to initiate legislation.

The staff members of the Ways and Means Committee viewed themselves as having a high "innovative" capability. Sixty-two percent of those Ways and Means staffers interviewed stated that part of their function was to initiate, innovate, and stimulate legislation. Only 43% of the staff members of the Senate Finance Committee shared such an orientation.

In the 1971-1972 session, for example, the staff of Ways and Means pushed through a measure requiring the governor to submit a five-year fiscal plan to the legislature. Although it had been recommended for a number of years by State Comptroller Arthur Levitt and "good government" groups, there was never any serious consideration given to such long-range planning until it was advocated by staff members of the Ways and Means Committee. The committee staff initiated a program of grants to county governments, with per capita income figured in for the first time in measuring local governments' ability to pay for services. The governor's budget bills were revised through amendments to break down "lump-sum" appropriations into specific program areas, as was recommended in a committee staff report prepared in October, 1971. For example, in the case of the State University of New York at Albany, which appeared as a single line in the budget, the appropriation was broken down to include program areas of instruction and departmental research, extension and public services, libraries, maintenance and operation of plant, food service, student aid, and other items. The governor's office, under pressure from the staff of the legislature, modified the budget process by eliminating the budget director's power to interchange the purpose of funds in the appropriations process. And in the legislatively initiated tax reform bill, the staff wrote 32 of the 35 articles.

It should be pointed out that about all the legislative staff can undertake during the session is an independent analysis from the legislative point of view of data and materials submitted by the various departments in support of or in opposition to various bills and a correlation of them with facts disclosed by hearings. After the legislature has adjourned, additional activity in the way of visits to agencies and field inspections can be managed to assist the legislature in the surveillance of administrative agencies. It is during the months when the legislature is not normally in session that more fundamental and less hurried studies can be made. The Ways and Means Committee, for example, has instituted a series of summer staff seminars in which staff members can conduct research programs and develop legislation. It was in one of these sessions, in the summer of 1971, that the staff undertook the development of a municipal bond bank for New York State. The staff first conducted a search of the literature, examined the historical background of earlier bond bank proposals in New York, reviewed proposals and legislation of other states, and instituted a feasibility study of a bond bank in New York.

The municipal bond bank concept is intended to help the small, unrated, or relatively low rated local government organizations. These governments rarely enter the credit market and, when they do, seek very limited amounts of capital. Thus, they are little known among investors and incur overhead costs high in relation to the dollar amount sought. The costs of employing the legal and financial advisors to guide a small issue through the maze of the bond market can be prohibitive to small governments. Small issues by small municipalities are less attractive to institutional investors than large issues because they are not easily traded. In addition, the secondary markets are also apathetic toward small issues by little-known municipalities. Another factor attesting the attractiveness of municipal bonds is the industrial diversification of the municipality. Many small municipalities do not have a very diversified economic base. Finally, the rating services often will not bother to rate small municipalities because they lack the detailed financial data and debt history required for a professional analysis.

The bond bank serves to mitigate this situation by assembling a group of local bond issues, then selling an issue equal to the total amount of the local issues, plus a sum for the reserve fund. With the proceeds of its bonds, the bank buys the local bonds. As towns pay them off from tax revenues, the bank retires its bonds. Thus, local governments would sell their bonds directly to the state (or its agency) and would save on interest and marketing costs. There would be no need for the local governments to seek ratings from any of the services, since the only rating that would matter would be that of the state agency. The single larger state bond issue would be attractive to investors and would overcome the diversification problem because the state bond issue would be backed by the diverse economies of the participating municipalities.

Staff members traveled to Vermont in the fall of 1971 to gather first-hand information on the workings of the Vermont Municipal Bond Bank and prepared a staff paper on the subject. Copies of the paper were sent to all relevant state agencies, to all local government organizations, and to the investment banking community requesting their reactions and comments. In December, the staff paper was presented to the Ways and Means Committee at a mini-session of the legislature and was released to the public. In January, after considering reactions from legislators and the involved groups, the staff of Ways and Means drafted legislation to create a municipal bond bank agency. During the months that followed, the staff held numerous discussions and meetings with members of the Housing Finance Agency, the Budget Division, the Office of Local Government, the investment bankers, and local government organizations. As a result of these meetings and a public hearing held in Albany on March 16, 1972, the bill was amended to include stronger guarantees for the bonds. The bill made its way through the legislative calendar and passed the Assembly on April 19 by a vote of 137 to 1. The bill was sent to the Senate, where it was passed on April 26 by a vote of 56 to 1. During April, the staff of Ways and Means met with staffers from the Senate Finance Committee, Governor Nelson Rockefeller's office, and Comptroller Arthur Levitt's office to negotiate and resolve problems and proposed changes. A chapter amendment embodying certain changes was prepared and was passed unanimously by the Assembly on May 4, 1972, and by the Senate on May 9. On June 9, the governor signed both bills into law as chapters 902 and 903 of the Laws of 1972. One of the staff members involved in the development of this piece of legislation discussed the innovative function of the staff in these terms:

> Oh, there's always been this talk about staff being "on tap, not on top" and "staff only advises, it doesn't decide," etc. But that's not our role here. We're not here like some encyclopedia that one has on hand and refers to occasionally. We're not just fact gatherers. We see it as part of our job to present alternatives to the legislator, to lay out things before him that he might want to do, to remind him sometimes of past promises and what he stands for, and, sometimes, to convince him of the worth of particular projects. That doesn't mean that we tell him what to do or that he's some kind of robot, with us in control. But a good staffer can point out executive inertia, formulate legislative remedies, and stimulate legislative activity.

Summary

With but few exceptions, there is general agreement that legislatures have declined in power vis-a-vis the executive, and that the decline in power is most visible in the decline of legislatures as initiators of legislation and innovators of public policy.[30] In a discussion of the declining role of Congress, for example, Samuel Huntington (1965: 23) has gone so far as to say that "the President now determines the legislative agenda of Congress almost as thoroughly as the British Cabinet set the legislative agenda of Parliament." Such statements have been so widely quoted and reprinted that their tentative nature is in danger of being forgotten.[31]

An examination of various staffs in the New York State Legislature shows that staff members see themselves as having innovative capabilities and that their work enabled the legislature to originate legislation, work out legislative ideas, and amend or modify proposals emanating from the executive branch or interest groups. These findings are important, since students of the legislative process occasionally look to expansion in professional staff as a means by which the institution can recover some of the capacity for policy initiation alleged to have been lost to the executive.

INFLUENCE

The term "influence" and its close ally "power" are among the classical concepts of political science. One writer (Ulmer, 1961: 332) has suggested that "content analysis of the political writings from Aristotle to the present would no doubt reveal power as the central concept around which attempts to explain politics have revolved." Although power and influence are distinguished by different writers, usages of the terms are by no means constant. As used in this analysis, "influence" is the more general term. A person may be said to have influence to the extent that he alters by persuasion the covert or overt behavior of others in accordance with his own intentions (the test is whether the behavior of others would have been different without the intervention of the man with influence). "Power" is the ability to employ force, i.e., to apply effective, coercive sanctions.

In this study, we are concerned with the "reputational" or "attributed" or "perceived" influence of staff members. Legislators, lobbyists, executive agency personnel, and staffers were asked about the importance of professional staff.[32] The advantages and disadvantages of such an approach were outlined by James G. March (1955: 455):

> Such a procedure has certain obvious advantages that should not be overlooked. In the first place, it is simple. The simplicity from the point of view of the observer is clear. The simplicity from the point of view of the respondent is less obvious, and strong reasons for anticipating considerable response difficulty can be found. However, so long as the response categories are relatively broad, no serious difficulty has been reported on this score by observers who have used this technique. In the second place, it taps unexpressed feelings and the implications of unobserved events. When overt behavior is observed over a time interval, there appear to be aspects of the influence pattern that are elusive.... By focusing on attributed power, it may be possible to distinguish real influence from pseudo-influence.

> While the introspective nature of this approach provides, at least potentially, a major source of its attractiveness, it also results in a major disadvantage. One has a certain hesitancy in accepting an individual's self-evaluation of personal motivation in view of the distortions, conscious and unconscious, that may be ordinarily anticipated.[33]

The problems raised by March were mitigated somewhat by the fact that we were dealing not only with staffers' assessments of their own influence, but also with the influence attributed to staff members by legislators, lobbyists, and administrative personnel. An attempt was also made to determine staff influence in various legislative decisions during the 1971-1972 session.

"Of all the sources of power in Albany today," said one member of the governor's staff, "the most nearly invisible—yet in some ways the most influential—is the legislative staff." J. Leiper Freeman (1965: 111-112), in a discussion of Congress, has argued the case for the influence capability of legislative staffs in the following way:

> Larger and more qualified staffs furnish committee leaders with information apart from the reports of the bureaucracy. They are also agents whose loyalties are more likely to be in the direction of committee leaders. Yet, in another sense, increased committee staffing does not eliminate the dependency of committee members upon others for information, but only transfers it from bureaucrats to committee staff experts. The sources of a congressman's dependency upon some kinds of specialists lie considerably beyond the need for committee staff help; they lie in the many competing demands upon legislators' time and in the complex variety of issues which they must attempt to resolve. Consequently, well-entrenched, well-trained, and astute committee staff members are often in quite favorable positions to be "powers behind the scenes" insofar as committee members transfer their dependency to them.

Legislators recognize the important role of the staff in the decision-making process (see Table 8). As one Republican assemblyman said:

TABLE 8
HOW LEGISLATORS ARE INFLUENCED IN THEIR VIEWS: LEGISLATIVE STAFF

Legislators' Views of Legislative Staff Influence	Total (n=51)	Assembly (n=38)	Senate (n=13)
Very influential	44%	45%	39%
Influential	52	54	42
Not influential	4	—	19
Total	100	99	100

These staff members don't have power. That is, as you know, reserved to the elected representatives of the people. But they do have influence, which results from the knowledge which they acquire and from the inevitable tendency of all busy persons to get rid of routine tasks which they think staff assistants will be competent to perform. Sometimes it turns out that the tasks are not routine at all but are in fact policy-determining.

Another assemblyman, considered to be a power in the chamber, put it much more colorfully:

There's an old joke about a man who claimed he made all his family's big decisions while his wife made the small ones. "My wife decides when we buy a new car, where we go on vacation, and how big an addition we put on the house," the man said. "I decide whether we recognize Red China."

The legislative staff is a bit like that wife. In its work, it may make decisions of greater impact on the day-to-day lives of the people of the State of New York than most of the acts of the legislature.

The response of administration officials also testifies to the role of the staff in strengthening the legislature. One of the major conclusions of our discussions with people in the executive branch was that, because of recent increases in legislative staffs, legislative influence in the live of the executive branch has become more complex, more subtle, and more detailed. If criticism is any indication, the staff has certainly achieved some success. Officials ranging from the governor to agency spokesmen have criticized the staff for meddling in administrative matters instead of concentrating on potential alternatives to major executive proposals. Yet, executive officials have gradually and grudgingly come to regard legislative staff as a force with which they must reckon. Nineteen of the twenty interviewed, members of agencies, the Division of the Budget, and the governor's staff, gave grudging praise to the competence and expertise of the legislative staff (see Table 9). As one member of the governor's staff stated:

As the legislature has added to its professional staff, it has become less and less, well, pliant is too strong a word, but less willing to go along. They've begun to initiate instead of just reacting to our proposals. The days of the rubber-stamp legislature are gone.

The staff is also a common target for informed Albany lobbyists, as Table 10 indicates.

TABLE 9
EXECUTIVE PERSONNEL'S VIEWS OF LEGISLATIVE STAFF INFLUENCE

Influence of Legislative Staff	Proportion of Executive Personnel Giving Response (n=20)
Very influential	55%
Influential	40
Not influential	5
Total	100%

TABLE 10
LOBBYISTS' VIEWS OF LEGISLATIVE STAFF INFLUENCE

Influence of Legislative Staff	Proportion of Lobbyists Giving Response (n=10)
Very influential	20%
Influential	70
Not influential	10
Total	100

As we noted earlier, contacts between the staff and interest group representatives are frequent, legitimate, and important. As a lobbyist pointed out:

A lot of lobbyists would rather talk to the staff than try to get in to see the members themselves. Staff members are more accessible than the legislators. They're going to be gathering the information anyway, so why not talk to them at the beginning. They're more expert in the subject matter, therefore they're more likely to understand your argument. And besides, the legislators and the staff people are so intertwined, so interdependent that talking to a staffer is just like talking to the legislator.

Staff members are also aware of their influence and their perceptions of their own importance closely coincide with the perceptions of the legislators, executive personnel, and lobbyists interviewed (see Table 11).

TABLE 11
PERCENTAGE OF STAFFERS VIEWING THEMSELVES AS INFLUENTIAL

Staff		Percentage of Staffers Giving Response
Ways and Means	(n=16)	100%
Senate Finance	(n=14)	86
Central Staff	(n=15)	80
Leadership Staffs	(n=17)	88

The difference increased professional staff has made in legislative operations was described by one member of Assembly Central Staff:

> We provide the legislature with the ability to review legislation in committee from a factual viewpoint. I'll never forget the first committee meeting I attended. It was one of the biggest shocks in my life. The counsel to the committee was from the chairman's home district and was usually in Albany one or two days a week. He wasn't around permanently, and he was never here during the summer. Well, at the meeting, there were about fifteen bills on the agenda and the counsel attempted to describe them and to state whether he was in favor of the bill or against it. The committee members asked him questions, and he couldn't answer them because he hadn't had enough time to study and examine them. They made their decision based on assumption. Things have changed now. We provide the staff services for the committees and assist their counsels. The facts are presented now and we can answer 80-90 percent of any of the questions raised. And when we don't know the answer we lay the bill over for a week until we find it. This has strengthened the committee system, reduced the number of bills going out of committee, and improved the quality of the bills sent to the floor.

An experienced Democratic senator evaluated the impact of the staff as follows:

> When the legislature depends on the executive agencies or private interest groups for research instead of relying on its own sources of

information, it makes its choices from the alternatives offered by the interest groups or the executive. Now we have an independent check because we have professional staff. They provide us with alternatives. The acquisition of correct information is the basis of sound public policy. The crux of the whole thing is to understand bills. The necessity to legislate implies the ability to understand what you are talking about. With adequate staff assistance, we are now able to do this as well as to come up with legislation of our own.

The potential influence of the staff is considerable indeed. It is a great deal easier to say that the staff plays an important political role in the legislature than to document precisely what that role is. The staff's influence is hard to isolate from other factors. An examination of the work of the Ways and Means Committee staff may illustrate the influence the staff can have.

In creating fiscal staffs, legislative leaders hoped to redress the imbalance between gubernatorial and bureaucratic power on the one hand and legislative power on the other. An important impetus for legislative modernization in New York was conflict with the executive branch.[34] In 1964, for the first time in many years, the Democrats gained control of the legislature. As one staffer described it, "When the Democrats took over the legislature, they sought to use it as a focus of opposition to the incumbent governor, and they thought it would be useful to further staff Assembly Ways and Means. Fiscal staffing was thought necessary in order to enhance legislative power."

Legislative reform gained prominence in the 1968 legislative campaign, and when the Republicans regained control of the Assembly[35] and elected Perry Duryea Speaker, he gave it top priority. The 1969-1970 Joint Legislative Committee on Legislative Fiscal Analysis and Review, chaired by Duryea, advised Ways and Means that it should review revenues as well as expenditures in the governor's budget.[36] One legislator stated that "Ways and Means was restructured to wage fiscal war on the governor."

When the 1971-1972 budget of $8.45 billion was received by the legislature, the Ways and Means Committee was equipped with both revenue and expenditure analysts. Their research found that the government's growth rate far exceeded revenue growth, and they informed Speaker Duryea "that the governor's revenue estimates could not possibly be met." The Ways and Means staff attacked the budget—with "a meat ax," the governor said—and on March 4, 1971, recommended cuts that eventually totaled $756 million.[37] One important facility was closed down, largely owing to staff work.[38] The Ways and Means Committee and the Assembly responded affirmatively to staff suggestions for budget cuts. Of 25 recommendations, 24 were accepted in precisely the form proposed by the staff. Savings of approximately $480,000,000 could be directly attributed to the fiscal staff, and an additional $157,000,000 in budget reductions was certainly an indirect consequence of its suggestions.[39]

Cuts in the 1972-1973 budget were forestalled in January, 1972, when Democratic votes were needed to pass the governor's $407,000,000 tax package. In return for their votes, Democrats demanded that spending for education and social programs not fall below given levels. The governor and Senate Majority Leader Earl Brydges agreed, but Assembly Speaker Perry Duryea only went along to a degree. The tax program went through. However, Duryea instructed the staff of Ways and Means to reorder priorities and to find additional funds for the Mental Hygiene Department. In a year of fiscal austerity, the staff found a way to provide an additional $10,000,000 to $20,000,000 for Mental Hygiene.

The 1972-1973 budget points to an indirect effect, primarily of a deterrent nature, that results from legislative staffing. One aim in expanding the staff, according to the staffers interviewed, was to promote greater fiscal alertness and responsibility by the executive. It was hoped that the very existence of a fiscal staff would encourage departments and agencies to budget more stringently—to pad less. Although accurate measurement is not possible, it does seem that executive anticipation of more intense legislative examination makes a difference. Of the twenty executive officials interviewed, seventeen stated that the cuts made in 1971 moved them to adopt a more cautious approach to the legislature in 1972. A budget official made the point quite explicitly:

> Last year the legislature tore the heart out of our budget proposals. They got a lot of publicity as economizers, especially Ways and Means. This year we cut the budget to the bare bones in anticipation of the staff's attack.

Agency representatives stated that they check with the legislative staff prior to formulating their budget requests and that they took greater pains in 1972 than in 1971 in preparing and justifying agency proposals in order to minimize their vulnerability. Members of the governor's staff and the budget officials interviewed also stated that their behavior had been affected by legislative staffing. Even before executive budget hearings, budget advisers stated that they cautioned agencies to cut items in anticipation of legislative staff scrutiny. The governor's advisers noted that during executive hearings they devoted particular attention to those areas most likely to receive critical staff examination. In fact, several legislators believed that the chief value of increasing staffing for the fiscal committees was not that it helped the legislature reduce appropriations, but rather that it encouraged the departments to budget more stringently.[40]

Reasons for Staff Influence

Legislators and staff members suggested several reasons to explain the influence of the staff. Table 12 shows the reasons given by respondents when they were asked why staff members were influential. Three of these merit further attention because of the number of times they received mention.

If, as Francis Bacon said, "knowledge is power," it seems that a good deal of the influence of the staff is seen to rest on the expertise of staff members. As the modern bureaucracy has grown, it has accumulated a "monopoly of skills" in critical areas of public policy.[41] The legislature has been faced with the choice of how to develop its own understanding of new policy problems. The trend toward the concentration of technical, specialized information in the executive branch and the resulting dependence of the legislature on the executive branch for much of its policy information has been clearly discernible. As one Democratic assemblyman noted:

> Undoubtedly one of the great contributing factors to the shift of influence from the legislative to the executive branch is the fact that we've been generous in providing them with experts and technically trained personnel but stingy in providing such personnel for ourselves.

TABLE 12
REASONS GIVEN FOR STAFF INFLUENCE*

Responses	Legislators (n=51)	Staffers (n=62)
Knowledge of field (expertise)	55%	61%
Tenure with legislature	10	16
Personal abilities	16	24
Specialization	39	61
Heavy burden on legislators	14	50
Information filter	47	53
Other	4	8

*Respondents gave multiple responses, therefore columns do not total 100 percent.

Legislators, then, realize that they need assistance in securing information and advice on pending legislation and recognize the expertise of the professional legislative staff. As one senator responded in explaining staff influence:

> Most of our 150 assemblymen and 57 senators come to Albany not as specialists in lawmaking but as politicians. The average member of the legislature has no time for research and few can afford to employ competent personal research assistants. It is no criticism of the committee members to say that, with few exceptions, they are not technical experts on fiscal policy or the state budget. That's why we turn to our staff. They have the expertise and the time to analyze an arcane document like the budget. The legislators just can't do it. Under the circumstances, it's all but certain that as time passes, the power of the staff will expand even further.

While staff expertise is viewed as a source of influence, it is also seen as a source of conflict. One legislator pointed up the problem when, after discussing staff influence because of their expertise, he went on to say:

> Legislators are predominantly lawyers and businessmen. They are elected to office not because they have necessarily mastered the art of government, but more because they have mastered the art of politics. Being successful and knowing it, many have tended to mistrust the professional staffer. Sometimes you hear reference to "the know-it-all" staff men.

The fact that many a legislator soon comes to know that he himself does not know it all serves only to aggravate the suspicion and the problem. Add to that the fact that one of the key objectives of many legislators is to stay in office, some members come to look upon professional staff members as potential rivals. Related to that, and equally important, is the fact that working with a staff member closely means revealing human weaknesses as well as political confidences—thus quite understandably legislators are more interested in loyalty than in knowledge and expertness.

Closely associated with staff expertise is specialization. A norm of behavior among legislative staffers is that they are expected to specialize and develop a subject-matter expertise.[42] Specialization and subject-matter expertise, then, are interrelated, since it is only through specialization that the staffer can come to know more about a subject than the legislators or other staff members. As Donald Matthews (1960: 97) noted, modern legislation is complex and technical and it comes before the legislature in a crushing quantity. Specialization increases skill, allows for subject-matter expertise, and decreases the average staffer's work load to something approaching manageable proportions.

Finally, legislators and staff members noted the influence of staff in terms of their responsibility for "editing," "compiling," "directing," "filtering," "sifting," and "interpreting" the flow of information to the legislature. Forty-seven percent of the legislators and 53% of the staffers interviewed explained the influence of the staff in such terms. Such references suggest certain aspects of communication theory as a means of understanding staff influence.

The legislative process is, among other things, a communications process. Each of the legislative stages, from formulation to passage, involves the conveyance, reception, and interpretation of information, questions and answers, attempts to persuade and prescribe. Actors in the process thus form a communications "net," and a person's or group's place in the net provides some indication of his role and his "weight" in the total process.

Staff people are not in a position to wield great power (unless they are acting for their bosses), but they have an advantage in their strategic position in the communications network. Staff members serve as the "gatekeepers" in what may be likened to a "two-step flow of communication" to the legislature. An examination of these two concepts might be in order before we proceed further.

It was the late Kurt Lewin (1947: 145) who applied the term "gatekeeper" to a phenomenon which is of considerable importance to students of mass communications.[43] In his last article Dr. Lewin pointed out that the traveling of a news item through certain communications channels was dependent on the fact that certain areas within the channels functioned as "gates." Carrying the analogy further, Lewin said that gate sections are governed by impartial rules or by "gatekeepers," and in the latter case an individual or group is "in power" for making the decision between "in" or "out." The legislative staffer is like a "gatekeeper" in that he holds a strategic location with respect to "the world outside" his group. Similarly, as we attempted to point out earlier, the selection of "information" for the legislators (like the selection of "news" for the newspapers) can often be quite subjective and reliant upon value-judgments based on the gatekeeper's own set of experiences, attitudes, and expectations.[44] It is this fact, that staff members are not neutral ciphers, that alarmed an assistant budget director:

> Certain staff members have become too influential. Last year, when we were discussing the tax program for New York City, we were dealing with [a Ways and Means staffer] and [an aide to the Senate

Majority Leader]. They were acting as if they had a personal stake in the thing. They represent themselves as just staff for their bosses, the legislative leaders. But they were dealing on their own; their own views were very much evident. I think the legislators are assuming a certain neutrality as the legislative leaders should have the facts presented to them. The legislators are being manipulated by the staff. Some of the staff members are acting like they're legislators.

The legislators, overloaded with messages, turn the processing of information over to the staff. The staff can allow information which supports their personal preferences to pass on to the legislators and cull out that which opposes their preferences.

Analysis of the process of decision-making during the course of an election campaign led the authors of *The People's Choice* (Lazarsfeld, Berelson, and Gaudet, 1948: 151) to suggest that the flow of mass communications may be less direct than was commonly supposed. It may be, they proposed, that influences stemming from the mass media first reach "opinion leaders" who, in turn, pass on what they read and hear to those of their everyday associates for whom they are influential. This hypothesis was called "the two-step flow of communication."

Subsequent studies, more specifically tailored to explore the phenomenon of opinion leadership, have elaborated upon the original findings and refined the original hypothesis. Research has been focused on the processes by which people come to decisions regarding public issues, change their food purchasing habits and habits of dress, and select the movies they attend.[45] In all of these matters, and presumably in others, many people appear to be more crucially influenced by specific other individuals than by pertinent mass communications. These specific others, or "opinion leaders," or "influentials" may serve a following of one, of three or four, or of somewhat more, but they typically do so in reference to only one topic (i.e., the fashion leader is not likely to be a marketing leader). "Opinion leaders and the people whom they influence are very much alike and typically belong to the same primary groups of family, friends, and co-workers."[46] The leader, however, is typically found to be more exposed than are his followers to media appropriate to his sphere of influence and to other sources of pertinent information to which the followers are not exposed.

Mass communication may enter this decision-making process at several points, but regardless of its port of entry, it is likely to become susceptible to the mediation of the opinion leader. It may, for example, provide the follower with information, define a point of view, or otherwise provide raw material which is later molded by the opinion leader. Or, after the follower has been influenced by the opinion leader, mass communication may provide material which the follower selectively attends or perceives to buttress his newly adopted opinion. For the opinion leader himself, wide exposure to mass communication provides information and points of view which he may or may not pass on to his less widely exposed followers.[47] The leader's occasions for mediation are multiple.

The hypothesis arouses considerable interest and its implications for understanding the role of the staff in the legislative process are intriguing. Majority rule within the legislature depends upon a narrowing process which ultimately permits decision in terms of aye or nay. Legislative staff members, in assembling data, are the liaison between the rather vague, inchoate demands for action and the persons officially charged with participating in the decision-making process. In a real sense, the staff acts as gatekeepers, as an intervening bureaucracy in a two-step flow of demands, requests, information, and so on between the members of the legislature and the network of advocates seeking legislative action. They serve as "opinion leaders," as an "attitude elite" in their areas of legislative specialization to whom the lawmakers turn for information and advice. They filter the competing demands for legislative attention and help decide who is to be granted access. They specialize in interpreting technical aspects in terms comprehensible to the legislator. Their function is to clarify, not to muddy the water further, and to aid in the limiting of choices within possible practical alternatives. In the process of selecting the "important" things out of the vast stream of communications from interest groups, constituents, the governor's office, executive agencies, and so on, the staff has the potential of exercising considerable influence on the legislator and his decisions. Their definition of "the issue" influences how the legislators act and what the issues are. A counsel to the governor pointed out, "Staff concerns tend to be, or become, legislators' concerns." A staff man made the same point, "What we feel is important ends up as what the legislature feels is important." Inherent in the work of the staff then are innumerable personal value-judgments which, while not prejudging the ultimate issues, shift the spotlight from the irrelevant or immaterial to what the staffer considers to be the centers of attention. As one senator noted, "In the process of selecting the 'important' things out of the vast amount of information available to us, the staff has quite a bit of influence on the senators and their decisions." Thus it seems that staff members can and do "pressure" legislators into taking action merely by the way they present the issues and the analysis. And they serve as an essential communications link between legislators and the outside world.

It seems then that the traditional concept of professional legislative staff as "neutral and objective instruments" inadequately reflects the reality of their participation in the legislative process. The obvious fact from our analysis of professional staffs in the New York State Legislature is that they are not merely "neutral agents devoid of values and providing purely objective data."[48] They are, inexorably, important participants in the legislative process in their own right, and their views have important implications for policy-making.

SUMMARY

It seems clear that a new approach to the study of legislative institutions is needed which will more adequately fuse the individual and his social setting and allow legislative units to be approached in terms of their systemic positions and roles. As Louis Froman has noted (1968: 524-525), "Propositions in organization theory may be very helpful in causal analysis of political institutions other than those usually included in public administration. The executive branch is by no means the only location of formal organizations which may have common features." Unfortunately, students of the legislative process cannot turn readily to public administration for insight or inspiration in dealing with the questions they need to address. In a sense, students of public administration have failed to meet their obligation to the less organizationally literate students of legislative institutions. From the research presented, it seems clear that public administration can offer some new insights into legislative structures and their environment. In addition, public administration and organization theory as applied to the study of legislative staffs may widen some traditional assumptions about the roles and functions of those structures.

In addition, if we consider administration to be a process as well as an academic discipline—that is, as a body of knowledge and techniques for the effective management of any enterprise—then it is needed in legislatures just as in other organizations. Legislatures need to be properly organized and managed. As Nigro and Nigro (1973: 6) have pointed out:

> In short, if they are to function satisfactorily, legislatures must constantly improve their own internal organization and procedures; their failure to do so accounts for much of today's dissatisfaction with lawmakers. Thus, looking at the legislature from the "inside," we find that it needs good administration.

Thus, legislatures could be assisted if they had systematic procedures by which to identify and give careful attention to significant proposals while giving less attention to unimportant proposals. Committees and individual legislators require professional staff; but how should these staffs be organized for doing the best possible job and what are the consequences of different organizational patterns?

It seems an obvious conclusion that legislatures ought to be a part of the study and practice of public administration. It is our hope that the shortcomings of this article may serve to stimulate more refined applications of the principles and precepts of public administration to the study of legislative institutions.

NOTES

1. Donald Herzberg and Jess Unruh, *Essays on the State Legislative Process* (New York: Holt, Rinehart, and Winston, 1970), esp. pp. 103-111.

2. In a recent compilation of recommendations from various reports, more pages were devoted to staff and services than to any other subject. Citizens Conference on State Legislatures, *Compilation of Recommendations Pertaining to Legislative Improvement in the Fifty States* (Kansas City, Mo.: The Conference, April 1967). See also John C. Wahlke, "Organization and Procedure" in Alexander Heard, ed., *State Legislatures in American Politics* (Englewood Cliffs, N. J.: Prentice-Hall, 1966). Surveys conducted in Maryland, Connecticut, New Jersey, Mississippi, Florida, Wisconsin, and Rhode Island also indicate widespread legislator agreement on the need for professional staff. See the Strengthening the Legislature series prepared by the Center for State Legislative Research and Service, Eagleton Institute of Politics, New Brunswick, New Jersey. For further statements along this line see Jess M. Unruh, Speaker, California Assembly, speech delivered at the Western Political Science Association Meeting, "Scientific Input to Legislative Decision Making," University of Utah, Salt Lake City, Utah, March 20, 1964; George H. Favre, "State Legislatures Brush at Cobwebs," *The Christian Science Monitor*, June 8, 1966; Albert J. Abrams, "Scapegoatism and the Legislatures," *State Legislatures Progress Report*, November 1965, supplement; Belle Zeller, ed., *American State Legislatures* (New York: Thomas Y. Crowell, 1954), pp. 159-162; James Nathan Miller, "Hamstrung Legislatures," *National Civic Review*, Vol. 54 (April 1965), p. 183; and Jess M. Unruh, "Science in Law-Making," *National Civic Review*, Vol. 54 (October 1965), pp. 467-469.

3. For discussions of Congress see, for example, Ernest S. Griffith, *Congress: Its Contemporary Role* (New York: New York University Press, 1951), ch. 7; John S. Saloma III, *Congress and the New Politics* (Boston: Little, Brown, 1969), ch. 7; and Joint Committee on the Organization of the Congress, *Final Report* pursuant to S. Con. Res. 2, 89th Congress, July 28, 1966, pp. 21-23, 36-42. With regard to state legislatures, see the Council of State Governments, *Mr. President ... Mr. Speaker* (Chicago: The Council, 1963); the Council of State Governments, *American State Legislatures in Mid-Twentieth Century* (Chicago: The Council, 1961); and Citizens Conference on State Legislatures, *The Sometimes Governments* (New York: Bantam, 1971).

4. For a review of the literature distinguishing between politics and administration, see Dwight Waldo, *The Administrative State* (New York: Ronald Press, 1948), pp. 106-114.

5. Charles McCarthy, for example, founder of a number of legislative service agencies in Wisconsin, was in the center of the public training movement from its inception. Rule 3 adopted by McCarthy for the Wisconsin drafting service read as follows: "The draftsman can make no suggestions as to the contents of the bill. Our work is merely clerical and technical. We cannot furnish ideas." Charles McCarthy, *The Wisconsin Idea* (New York: Macmillan, 1912), p. 197. See also Edward A. Fitzpatrick, *McCarthy of Wisconsin* (New York: Columbia University Press, 1944).

6. See Herbert A. Simon, *Administrative Behavior* (New York: Macmillan, 1957), pp. 45-60.

7. See the description of Floyd B. Reeves' schema in Paul H. Appleby, *Policy and Administration* (University: University of Alabama Press, 1949), pp. 17-18.

8. For a more detailed treatment of this tendency among political scientists, see Morley Segal, "The Role and Functions of the Legislative Staff in the California Assembly" (unpublished Ph. D. dissertation, Claremont Graduate School, 1965), esp. pp. 83-107. For a critique of the general tendency of American students of organization to conceive "staff" as a "neutral and inferior instrument," see Robert T. Golembiewski, "Toward the New Organization: Some Notes on 'Staff,' " *Midwest Journal of Political Science*, Vol. 5 (August 1961), pp. 237-259.

9. Max M. Kampelman, "The Legislative Bureaucracy: Its Response to Political Change, 1953," *Journal of Politics*, Vol. 16 (August 1954), p. 549.

10. The major source of data for this study is a body of 148 interviews conducted by one of the authors with individuals involved in the legislative process in New York State. Most of the interviews used in this study were conducted in Albany between July 1971 and February 1972 as part of a larger study of legislative staffing in New York completed in partial fulfillment of the requirements for a doctorate at the State University of New York at Albany. Of the 148 interviews, 62 were with members of the staffs of the Assembly Ways and Means Committee, the Senate Finance Committee, Assembly Central Staff, and the legislative leaders (speaker, president pro tempore of the Senate, and the minority leaders), 51 were with legislators, 20 with members of the executive branch (members of the governor's staff, budget officials, program officers, and assistant commissioners in various agencies, etc.), 10 with lobbyists, and 5 with journalists. The interviews were of the focused type. Certain key questions, all open-ended, were asked of all respondents holding similar positions. But the interview was kept very flexible in order to permit particular topics to be explored with those individuals best equipped to discuss them. Notes were not taken during the interview but were transcribed immediately afterward. Unattributed quotations in the text, therefore, are as nearly verbatim as the author's power of immediate recall could make them. These techniques were used in the belief that they encouraged what the author believes to be the most essential condition of successful interviewing of legislative elites—rapport between interviewer and respondent. See Balutis (1973).

11. The staff responses utilized to define this function were those that discussed their role in investigating, researching, scheduling, editing, compiling, and distributing much of the information on which legislative decisions are based. Their tasks included work on legislation and administrative oversight. Intelligence is, therefore, defined as the action of gathering, processing, interpreting, and communicating the technical and political information needed in the decision-making process.

12. H. Alexander Smith, "Information and Intelligence for Congress," *Annals of the American Academy of Political and Social Science*, Vol. 289 (September 1953), p. 114.

13. David B. Truman, *The Governmental Process* (New York: Alfred A. Knopf, 1951), p. 334.

14. Saloma, *Congress and the New Politics*, p. 209.

15. For a discussion of this point, see William J. Siffin, *The Legislative Council in the American States* (Bloomington: Indiana University Press, 1959), pp. 218-223.

16. The question asked was, "What does your job consist of—what do you do here?"

17. Smith, "Information and Intelligence for Congress," pp. 116-117.

18. J. G. Miller, "Information Input, Overload, and Psychopathology," *American Journal of Psychiatry*, Vol. 116 (1960), pp. 695-704.

19. David Brinkley opened a November 1965 NBC-TV News Special Report, entitled "Congress Needs Help," standing next to mountainous piles of papers that passed through a typical congressman's office in a single session. Congressmen utilize their legislative assistants, office staff, committee staff, the Congressional Research Service, and staff assistance from other sources to help them process this glut of information.

20. See Richard F. Fenno, Jr., "The House Appropriations Committee as a Political System: The Problem of Integration," *American Political Science Review*, Vol. 56 (June 1962), pp. 310-324, and Robert K. Merton, *Social Theory and Social Structure* (Glencoe, Ill.: Free Press, 1957), pp. 26-29.

21. On the idea of subgroup as used here, see Harry M. Johnson, *Sociology* (New York: Harcourt Brace Jovanovich, 1960), ch. 3.

22. Interviews conducted with Assembly Central Staff personnel and Ways and Means staffers provided the basis for this finding. In the Senate, staffers serving the Finance Committee reported contact with the staffs of other standing committees. Supplementary interviews focusing on each interstaff contact were held with five staff members from the Health, Education, and Judiciary Committees.

23. The legislative leadership has established several informal methods of coordination and control over the standing committees. They are ex officio members of all committees and attend meetings occasionally. Leadership staffers usually monitor committee meetings and hearings, according to the legislators interviewed.

24. A certain amount of cooperation has been built into the system through the use of a dual reference procedure. Bills involving an expenditure of funds are referred to a fiscal committee after they have been considered and reported by a subject matter committee.

25. Interviews with staff members of Assembly Ways and Means and those of Senate Finance indicated some tension between the two committees, both in information sharing and in competition for public recognition.

26. Once again, the literature that does exist deals with Congress, pointing out the lack of concern with state legislatures. See Freeman (1965); Richard F. Fenno, Jr., *The Power of the Purse* (Boston: Little, Brown, 1966), ch. 6 and 7; and James A. Robinson, *Congress and Foreign Policy Making* (Homewood, Ill.: Dorsey Press, 1962), ch. 5 and 6.

27. For a discussion of a similar case at the federal level, see Elias Huzar, *The Purse and the Sword: Control of the Army by Congress through Military Appropriations, 1933-1950*, (Ithaca, N.Y.: Cornell University Press, 1950), pp. 102-103, 348.

28. For examples of works in political science which refer to the term but fail to

define it, see the following: Robert A. Dahl, *Who Governs?* (New Haven: Yale University Press, 1961); David B. Truman, *The Congressional Party* (New York: John Wiley, 1959); John D. Montgomery, *The Politics of Foreign Aid* (New York: Frederick A. Praeger, 1962); and James A. Robinson, *Congress and Foreign Policy-Making* (Homewood, Ill.: Dorsey Press, 1962).

29. The areas covered by such legislation ranged over environmental protection, consumer credit, powers of grand juries, freedom of information, the hepatitis outbreak and blood donors, and the state alcoholic programs, as well as many other fields.

30. See James J. Heaphey, "Technical Assistance in the Administration of Legislatures: Problems of Theory and Concepts." Presented at the annual meeting of the American Society for Public Administration, New York, March 1972, p. 7.

31. Heaphey, "Technical Assistance in the Administration of Legislatures," pp. 7-10.

32. The questions utilized were; Do you think the members of the legislative staff have much influence on policy-making in the legislature? Who? Under what conditions?

33. For a further discussion of the drawbacks of this approach, see Thomas J. Anton, "Power, Pluralism, and Local Politics," *Administrative Science Quarterly*, Vol. 7 (March 1963), pp. 427-457, and Nelson Polsby, "Three Problems in the Analysis of Community Power," *American Sociological Review*, Vol. 24 (December 1959), pp. 796-803.

34. Frequently conflict spurs legislative modernization. The establishment of a special legislative budget committee in California, for example, resulted from sharp antagonisms between the legislature and the governor. See D. Jay Doubleday, *Legislative Review of the Budget in California* (Berkeley: University of California Institute of Governmental Studies, October 1967), p. 36.

35. The Republicans had regained a majority of the Senate in 1966, but the Assembly remained under the control of the Democrats until 1968.

36. See the Report of the Joint Legislative Committee on Legislative Fiscal Analysis and Review, New York State Legislature, March 31, 1970.

37. In New York, as in other states, the legislature has practical control over a relatively small portion of total expenditures, since the financing of a number of programs is provided by formulas and continuing appropriations. Ordinarily the budget bill reported by the finance committees and enacted by the legislature is quite similar to the one introduced on behalf of the governor. Against this background, bearing in mind the limits of legislative control of state expenditures, the achievements of the staff are marked.

38. This analysis of staff recommendations is based on written memoranda and studies prepared by the staff and submitted to the Ways and Means Committee. Documents considered included only those which either explicitly made recommendations or presented alternatives in such a manner that staff preference was evident. It was impossible to account for recommendations communicated verbally. Thus, whatever bias exists would tend to understate the impact of the staff.

39. For a comparison of staff impact in California, see the reports of the Legislative Analyst, summarized in Doubleday, *Legislative Review of the Budget in California*, p. 81.

40. Doubleday, *Legislative Review of the Budget in California*, p. 95.

41. For a perceptive interpretation of the tendencies toward monopoly of skill

and monopoly of power in modern bureaucracy, see Reinhard Bendix, "Bureaucracy and the Problem of Power," *Public Administration Review*, Vol. 5 (Summer 1945), pp. 194-209.

42. Most summary studies of legislatures treat specialization only incidentally. See, for example, Galloway (1953: 315); Roland A. Young, *The American Congress* (New York: Harper, 1958), p. 107; Stephen K. Bailey and Howard D. Samuel, *Congress at Work* (New York: Henry Holt, 1952), pp. 203, 342ff.; and Bertram M. Gross, *The Legislative Struggle* (New York: McGraw-Hill, 1953), p. 388. Yet Donald Matthews found in his study of United States senators that they recognize and defer to the specialists among them, and that this custom gets their work done more efficiently. See Matthews (1960: 95-97).

43. The conceptual underpinnings of "gatekeeper" studies can be found in particular among those studies of human behavior which take place among the professions and within bureaucratic institutions. The most helpful analytic schemes have come from Kurt Lewin's social channel and field theories *(Field Theory in Social Science*, Dorwin Cartwright, ed., [New York: Harper, 1951]), Robert K. Merton's, among others, discussion of role behavior within reference groups *(Social Theory and Social Structure* [New York: Free Press, 1957]), and Bruce H. Westley's and Malcolm S. MacLean, Jr.'s model for communication research ("A Conceptual Model for Communications Research," *Journalism Quarterly*, Vol. 34 [Winter 1957], pp. 31-38).

44. For a further discussion of this point, see David Manning White, "The 'Gate Keeper': A Case Study in the Selection of News," *Journalism Quarterly*, Vol. 27 (Fall 1950), pp. 383-390, and Walter Gieber, "News Is What Newspapermen Make It" in Lewis Anthony Dexter and David Manning White, eds., *People, Society and Mass Communications* (New York: Free Press, 1964).

45. For a further discussion on the "two-step flow" hypothesis, see Elihu Katz and Paul F. Lazarsfeld, *Personal Influence: The Part Played by People in the Flow of Mass Communications* (Glencoe, Ill.: Free Press, 1955); Robert K. Merton, "Patterns of Influence: A Study of Interpersonal Influence and Communications Behavior in a Local Community," in Paul F. Lazarsfeld and Frank N. Stanton, eds., *Communications Research 1948-49* (New York: Harper, 1948), pp. 180-219; and Bernard B. Berelson, Paul F. Lazarsfeld, and William N. McPhee, *Voting: A Study of Opinion Formation in a Presidential Campaign* (Chicago: University of Chicago Press, 1954).

46. Elihu Katz, "The Two-Step Flow of Communication: An Up-to-Date Report on an Hypothesis," *Public Opinion Quarterly*, Vol. 21 (Spring 1957), p. 77.

47. Joseph P. Klapper, *The Effects of Mass Communication* (New York: Free Press, 1960), p. 33.

48. Dale Vinyard, *Congress* (New York: Scribner's, 1968), p. 102.

REFERENCES

Advisory Commission on Intergovernmental Relations (1967) Fiscal Balance in the American Federal System. Washington, D.C.: The Commission.

BALUTIS, A. P. (1973) "Professional staffing in the New York State Legislature: an exploratory study." Ph.D. dissertation. State University of New York at Albany.

BAUER, R., I. de SOLA POOL, I. and L. A. DEXTER (1963) American Business and Public Policy: The Politics of Foreign Trade. New York: Atherton Press.
DAHL, R. A. (1957) "The concept of power." Behavioral Science 2 (July): 201-215.
DIMOCK, M. E. (1945) "Administrative efficiency in a democratic polity," in New Horizons in Public Administration: A Symposium. University: Univ. of Alabama Press.
DOWNS, A. (1967) Inside Bureaucracy. Boston: Little, Brown.
FORRESTER, J. W. (1962) "Managerial decision-making," in M. Greenberger (ed.) Computers and the World of the Future. Cambridge, Mass.: MIT Press.
FREEMAN, J. L. (1965) The Political Process: Executive Bureau-Legislative Committee Relations. New York: Random House.
FROMAN, L. A. (1968) "Organization theory and the explanation of important characteristics of Congress." American Political Science Rev. 62 (June): 518-526.
GALLOWAY, G. B. (1953) The Legislative Process in Congress. New York: Thomas Y. Crowell.
HATTERY, L. and S. HOFHEIMER (1954) "The legislators' source of expert information." Public Opinion Quarterly 15 (Fall): 300-303.
HUITT, R. K. (1964) "Congressional reorganization: the next chapter." Presented at the annual meeting of the American Political Science Association, Chicago.
HUNTINGTON, S. P. (1965) "Congressional responses to the twentieth century" in D. B. Truman (ed.) The Congress and America's Future. Englewood Cliffs, N. J.: Prentice-Hall.
JENNINGS, R. E. and M. MILSTEIN (1970) Educational Policy Making in New York State with Emphasis on the Role of the State Legislature. U. S. Department of Health, Education and Welfare, Office of Education, Bureau of Research.
KATZ, D. and R. L. KAHN (1966) The Social Psychology of Organizations. New York: John Wiley.
KAUFMAN, H. (1956) "Emerging conflicts in the doctrines of public administration." American Political Science Rev. 50 (December): 1057-1073.
KOVENOCK, D. (1964) "Communications and influence in Congressional decision-making." Paper presented at the annual meeting of the American Political Science Association, Chicago.
LASSWELL, H. D. and A. KAPLAN (1950) Power and Society. New Haven: Yale Univ. Press.
LAZARSFELD, P. F., B. BERELSON, and H. GAUDET (1948) The People's Choice. New York: Columbia Univ. Press.
LEWIN, K. (1947) "Channels of group life." Human Relations 1: 143-153.
LOCKHARD, D. (1966) "The state legislator" in A. Heard (ed.) State Legislatures in American Politics. Englewood Cliffs, N. J.: Prentice-Hall.
MARCH, J. G. (1955) "An introduction to the theory and measurement of influence." American Political Science Rev. 49 (June): 431-451.
MATTHEWS, D. R. (1960) U. S. Senators and Their World. New York: Vintage.
MELLER, N. (1967) "Legislative staff services: toxin, specific or placebo for the legislature's ills." Western Political Quarterly 20 (June): 381-389.
——— (1965) " 'Legislative behavior research' revisited: a review of five years' publications," Western Political Quarterly 18 (September): 776-793.
MILBRATH, L. W. (1963) The Washington Lobbyists. Chicago: Rand-McNally.
NIGRO, F. A. and L. G. NIGRO (1973) Modern Public Administration. New York: Harper & Row.

PATTERSON, S. C. (1970) "The professional staffs of congressional committees." Administrative Science Quarterly 15 (March): 22-38.
PEABODY, R. L. (1963) "Organization theory and legislative behavior: bargaining, hierarchy and change in the U.S. House of Representatives." Presented at the annual meeting of the American Political Science Association, New York.
POSCHMAN, E. S. (1970) "The images of organization, pluralism, and community in American social science literature on the legislature." Ph.D. dissertation. University of California (Berkeley).
REDMAN, E. (1973) The Dance of Legislation. New York: Simon & Schuster.
ROSENTHAL, A. (1973) "Contemporary research on state legislatures: from individual cases to comparative analysis," in Political Science and State and Local Government. Washington, D.C.: American Political Science Association.
SIMON, H. A. (1965) The Shape of Automation for Men and Management. New York: Harper and Row.
ULMER, S. (1961) Introductory Readings in Political Behavior. Chicago: Rand McNally.
WALKER, J. L. (1969) "The diffusion of innovations among the American states." American Political Science Rev. 63 (September): 880-899.
WHITE, L. D. (1945) New Horizons in Public Administration. University: Univ. of Alabama Press.
――― (1945) "Legislative responsibility for the public service," in New Horizons in Public Administration: A Symposium. University: Univ. of Alabama Press.
WILLOUGHBY, W. F. (1934) Principles of Legislative Organization and Administration. Washington, D.C.: Brookings.

ALAN P. BALUTIS *is assistant professor of political science at the State University of New York at Buffalo. He served on the staff of the New York State Constitutional Convention and the Joint Legislative Committee on Fiscal Analysis and Review, following work as a researcher for the National Legislative Conference. He received his doctorate from the State University of New York at Albany, where he was co-director of the New York State Internship Program and Project Officer of the Comparative Development Studies Center.*

JAMES J. HEAPHEY *is professor of public administration and director of the Comparative Development Studies Center. He is the author of numerous articles in professional journals and was editor of* Spatial Dimensions of Development Administration *(Duke University Press, 1971). He is currently conducting research on the role of legislatures in development and on organizational aspects of American state legislatures. Professors Balutis and Heaphey are co-editors of* Legislative Staffing: A Comparative Perspective, *to be published by Sage/Halsted-Wiley this fall.*

NOTES

NOTES

NOTES